THE CRUNCH

PAT TOOMAY

THE CRUNCH

First Edition published 1975 by Norton.

Copyright © 1975, 2013 by Pat Toomay

ISBN: 978-1-5040-2963-6

Distributed in 2016 by Open Road Distribution
180 Maiden Lane
New York, NY 10038
www.openroadmedia.com

for *Seth*

Contents

Illustrations appear between pages 96 and 97

"When smashing monuments, save the pedestals—
they always come in handy."

Stanislaw J. Lec

1

THE ORDEAL
OF A ROOKIE

June, 1970. I sit sweltering and sweating in my underwear; it is hot and the crickets have gone berserk. The oak trees in back of the house are infested with hungry seventeen-year locusts—cicadas—millions of them flying from limb to limb producing a continuous, shrill, whirring sound. The inaugural of another steamy Virginia summer.

Today was my second official workout day according to Dallas Cowboy off-season workout plans. I wake up when the cicadas start buzzing, eat, go to work out, and come home. I thought it would be more fun than this.

This morning I made the quiet drive down the Potomac, across the river, and into town to Fort Lesley J. McNair. Fort McNair is a traditional army installation—crisp uniforms, manicured lawns, and plenty of senior officers. I was a bit hesitant going in, as I am an Air Force kid with long hair and I had never ventured onto an army base before. I found the base gym, went in, and downstairs to dress. The weight room was locked, so I proceeded back upstairs to ask the attendant for the key. As I came up the stairs I overheard the end of a conversation.

"You want to tell someone to get a haircut? Try the kid in the weight room."

I stepped into the office as his words vaporized.

"Major, you talking about me?"

"I . . . yeah . . . you're a big ol' boy aren't you?"
Yes.

I worked the weights and then ran down along the river. It was a nice day to be out running; a midmorning breeze rustled off the Potomac, an easy, cool breeze. . . . I made the mistake, however, of sporting a Cowboy T-shirt for the workout; consequently I was stopped every hundred yards by inquisitive grounds keepers, staff officers, etc.

Preparation. The workout program is one of graduated difficulty and intensity, divided into work periods each lasting a week. The first week consists of running two miles per day and performing assorted calisthenics. It's not bad, but as the weeks progress you are required to get out the stopwatch and run distances for time: 220's, 440's, 880's, miles and multimiles. The closer the departure for training camp looms, the more frenzied the pace. The culmination of the program is the aerobic twelve-minute test; upon arrival at camp you are required to run a mile and one-half in twelve minutes.

My efforts in the past three months to gain weight have turned out very well. I needed an additional twenty pounds to become an effective National Football League defensive end, and now I have it. The next step is getting that bulk into some semblance of working order.

I have given up on Fort McNair as my workout grounds because of infinite hassle and lack of sympathy (their thinking was that the rigors of training camp are worth all the resulting bread; I argued that the bread was not necessarily forthcoming regardless of the intensity of the training). The new training site is my high-school alma mater, Edison High. They have a track to run on, and all my old coaches are available to chat with, so it shouldn't be unpleasant.

I sail along.

This third week requires a three-quarter-mile run for time, plus a couple of 440's at ninety seconds per lap. My

handy instruction chart emphasizes the sentence "Strive
for these times," which I misread initially as "Stride for
these times." A stride, however, does not yield the prescribed times, as I have discovered this week. A strive is
one gear up from a stride; realizing that, I shouldn't have
any problem making time from now on.

We had an off-season program similar to this one while I
was at Vanderbilt. The difference is that the Vanderbilt
program was utterly impossible to carry out (it consisted of
a mile trot to warm up, assorted exercises, ten 220's at full
tilt, and a half-mile jog, all topped off by a six-minute mile
run—the program defeated you mentally). Dallas coach
Tom Landry's is at least in the realm of possibility "if you
have the guts." Unfortunately, my guts tighten up at even
the suggestion of running, so I strive along, trying not to
tax my lungs.

Can't sleep this first night of summer; thunder mingles
outside my window. Tomorrow I have to go to Dallas, for I
am having deep problems with the army. They want me.
Fortunately, the Dallas Cowboys' antidraft tactics are
much more complex and effective than those of the most
skilled and dedicated college students. The first step is to
change one's residence. I was scheduled to take the draft
physical in Fairfax, Virginia, in May—I was in Nashville in
school at the time, so I changed to a Nashville address. I
am due to take the physical next week in Nashville, so
now I am off to Dallas for another residence change. Addresses and airline tickets are courtesy of the Cowboy office. Since each postponement buys approximately one
month, my physical will be moved to August. It's apparently true that if I can play for the Cowboys, no army. If
not . . .

Home finally. Six hours in planes and airports, jostled
and shoved, but the trip was worth it.

Down in Dallas I spent the day with the main man for

problems of this nature, and any other problems for that matter, Gil Brandt. Gil is the Player Personnel Director; he negotiates contracts, signs free agents, and can apparently talk anyone into anything. I had negotiated my contract without the benefit of a lawyer and I was concerned with how I came out.

"Gil, really now, no bullshit, how much better could I have done if I had gotten an attorney?"

"Pat, you got the best deal possible," Gil bullshitted.

It was hopeless talking to the guy, but he did say one straight thing: "All our boys seem to flunk their draft physicals. . . . I can't figure it out." A shake of the head, a wry smile; obviously it was worth the two hundred dollars it cost them to fly me down. To reiterate, if I can play the game, it won't be for Uncle Sam.

I quietly proceed. June passes and training camp is suddenly very close.

——————

July. I am leaving early for camp. Today is the seventh and we're not due in California until the tenth. The plan is to drive my car to Dallas, where it will be readily available whatever happens, and then to fly out from there.

I made it to Dallas early Friday only to find that there was a potential players' strike and the departure date had been changed to Monday. It had been hot driving down from Washington, extremely hot. Lulled and dulled, I was greeted here by draft and accommodation problems. The draft board was quenched with a phone call, and Gil Brandt, that man for all reasons, found me a room in the Hilton Inn. However, this is my third day in a strange town and I am bored, not to mention scared. Before I left home I overheard a telephone conversation between my father and his brother, with my father expressing confidence in my success. It struck me then that for the first time I am confronted with a failure situation—an opportunity to fall right on my face. I had never considered the possibility before. I always supposed it might happen, but the thought was tucked into the back of my mind. Previously I always had some indication of the ground I was treading; with the Cowboys there is so much garbage to transcend it's difficult to determine a starting point.

I don't know quite how I would take being cut. Training camp looms as an ultimate test; it's what I've been reaching for my entire athletic life without really realizing it as a possible culmination/end. Where your future depends on how you come off to some semi-literate coach, the only way seems to be to perform, to keep your mouth shut, and to hope for the best.

The plane leaves tomorrow morning at 10:30, and it all begins.

The first day. The airline ticket was marked LAX and we dropped into Los Angeles International right on time. I was making the quarter-mile trek to baggage claim when someone tapped me on the shoulder.

"Cowboys?"

"Yes."

"What in the hell do we do?"

The inquiry came from a wiry, wide-eyed six-footer. His lower jaw hung helplessly open, exposing a dull set of capped teeth; he appeared to be in a state of shock. Also: he was subtly freckled from the backs of his hands to the top of his head; his skullcap freckles were visible because there was no hair.

"Well," I said, trying to be logical, "I guess we pick up our luggage and find a bus to Thousand Oaks."

The Cowboy business manager found us, and about forty other prospects, and directed the group to the chartered buses out front. My new friend and I settled in for the bus ride. We were both sweating. My friend's name is Cliff Harris, and he is a free-agent defensive back from Ouachita Baptist College.

"Where?"

"Ouachita," he repeated. "It's in Arkadelphia, Arkansas."

I mentioned to Cliff that he looked a bit startled in the airport.

"I've never been west," he said. "I've never been anywhere."

"What do you think about all this?" I asked.

"I don't know," he muttered.

I didn't know either. We bumped on out to California Lutheran College.

The campus is several miles from Thousand Oaks proper, small but clean; our rooms are the same. I've counted close to eighty people this afternoon, every one a rookie. In a week forty-five veterans are scheduled to come in; out of this melange a forty-man active squad will emerge in September. The odds are staggering.

Neal Smith is here, an ex-Commodore like myself. The highlight of our college careers was being selected to play in the Blue–Gray Endurance Classic down in Montgomery, Alabama. The object of the game was to see if you could endure a week of your Christmas vacation in the Whitley Hotel, downtown Montgomery. Neal revealed his perseverance early. The first night we were there he became inebriated and threw a stack of folding chairs down into the lobby . . . one at a time. Neal is a bit nervous out here, biting his nails, worried that he won't last. Like Cliff he is a free-agent defensive back; Gil Brandt claims he has speed problems.

I feel a wash of confidence for some reason—skinny, hopefully quick, moving better than the bigger fellows—of course we haven't been on the field yet! My roommate of unknown duration is a black by the name of Calvin Stith. He is from Winston-Salem State University and downtown

Washington, D. C., an easy-to-get-along-with type, a fellow defensive end—very fast. I don't feel like analyzing my competition at this time.

Steve Kiner, All-World linebacker from the University of Tennessee, is here also. He used to upset me at Vanderbilt with his considerate comments about our football team: "Playing Vanderbilt is like having an off-week," he often said. To prove it Steve would play the first half, then appear in his street clothes for the second—grinning immensely. He has more raw nerve than anyone I have ever encountered; either that or he is incredibly ignorant. Early in our senior season Tennessee drubbed Alabama. The headline in the Nashville paper read: "Bear draws praise from Kiner." Apparently Steve went into the Alabama locker room immediately after the game and told Bear Bryant that his boys didn't know what it meant to wear those crimson jerseys anymore. "But," quoth Steve, "you're still the greatest in my book and I'd play for you anytime." Coach Bryant's comments were not reported. Kiner is playing the martyr here: sulking, eating alone, not speaking. He irks the hell out of me.

The veterans are collectively bargaining right now for a number of things, and in the process have upset the owners. The owners have consequently locked the players out of camp. I'm not sure at this point what will happen, but I do know one thing; I don't care if they never show up.

Today was orientation day: taking physicals, getting a time in the forty-yard dash, and then doing the weight program. All that was just this morning, and I'm beginning to wonder what the hell I'm doing here. The afternoon was spent on that damn twelve-minute test. I ran the forty in five seconds flat, which is fair to good, got through the weight program okay, and made the appointed mile and one-half in the allotted twelve minutes.

Cliff fared well in the early rounds also. My airport reaction on first seeing him was . . . goddamn, professional football players are supposed to be big! At 6 feet 0 inches, 185 pounds, Cliff is an average-sized defensive back, but that 185 pounds is well placed. He has a triangular upper body—broad shoulders, washboard gut, no hips. For speed and drive—thin legs, and a large, horizontal ass. He is built like a thoroughbred who's been pulling the hay wagon . . . and he's got all that good speed too.

We were thankful to complete the day. Five or six guys never got out of the doctor's office. If you are any kind of medical risk, you go home; this eliminates lawsuits from injured rookies who would not have normally made the team.

I find myself resenting the attitude the people here take toward the rookies, particularly the fringe people. The physicals were handled with the finesse of a cattle roundup; the front-office types treat you as they would a headache; and the equipment manager treats you like you were a pain in his ass.

Tonight we had our first meeting. Coach Landry told us, among other things, that he had devoted his life to Christ. The group shuddered until he reassured us that a firm belief in God was not a prerequisite for making the club; however, a firm belief in Tom Landry is. A few more words from his opening spiel: "We want everyone to look the same." I had discovered that earlier. Ernie Stautner, the defensive line coach, informed me that my hair, which had been cut four days before, needed cutting again (which I proceeded to do immediately). Tom also mentioned that it was essential to be clean-shaven. This didn't mean much to the white men in the group, all were clean-shaven, but for the blacks it was a major hurdle. My roomie had had his moustache since he was thirteen years old . . . off it came. "To play for the Cowboys you've got to fit a certain niche." I am wondering if my conception of my niche fits their conception of my niche. Tomorrow will be niche-conception day. Other essential particulars:

Pills: Take three yellow ones and four blue ones at all meals. *Duh.*

The daily schedule runs something like this:

7:30 A.M.	Breakfast (mandatory)
9:45–10:00	Isometric warm-up
10:00–10:15	Specialty period (kickers only)
10:15–11:45	Practice
12:30–12:45	Lunch
3:00– 3:15	Isometrics
3:15– 3:30	Specialty again
3:30– 5:00	Practice
5:00– 5:30	Weights? *Right.*
6:30– 6:45	Dinner
7:30– 9:30	Team meeting
11:00 P.M.	Check those beds

The schedule of fines is interesting too:

Sprained ankle, no tape	$250
Violation of curfew	75
15 minutes late	100
next 45 minutes	50
Late for meeting	50
Late for meal	50
Overweight, per pound	25
Gambling	250

All fines double on the second offense.

Today I find that our niche conceptions are not jiving. Being an offensive guard was hardly my intention and that's where I was at this morning's practice. Fortunately, I fouled up one of Coach Jim Myers' elaborate drills and he banished me to the defense as being incompetent. Relief. To date I have not formed a lofty opinion of offensive line coach Myers; he is disorganized, he snaps at the players, and he has never played a down of professional football. Myers seems to be picking on one player in particular—John Fitzgerald. Fitzgerald, a large, pleasant sort, played in the defensive line for Boston College and he is now trying to make the difficult switch to offensive guard.

On more than one occasion Coach Myers has grabbed Fitz by the face mask and slammed him forcefully across the earhole with his free hand. Poor Fitz is at a loss. The consensus of opinion calls for an ass-kicking, but John is quick to point out that beating on a coach is not the quickest way to make an NFL team.

Ernie Stautner is my mentor, thank God. I would hate to be in the hands of someone like Myers. Ernie has many of the characteristics of Vanderbilt's defensive line coach, George Bernhardt; they are both stocky, seemingly easygoing, with sound knowledge of the game and how to coach it. Ernie has been voted into the Pro Football Hall of Fame, and it is rumored that when he played, he was a total maniac. You'd never know it to be around him.

Mornings are tough. I can't begin to explain the pain and trauma of getting out of bed, and then the yearning for that mattress that hits as you leave the room. My left arm is swollen, my hands are balloons, my legs don't want to function, and my forehead is pulp (that bastard equipment man fitted my helmet like a Robert Hall suit). I need to sleep.

The object of psychological fixation off the field is your bed. You count the minutes until you can crawl back into the rack. On the field, the fixation is on liquid. The Conejo Valley is hot and dry, with a stiff breeze blowing most of the afternoon. The breeze sops the moisture right out of your mouth. It feels as if you are chewing cotton; breathing is difficult, talking is impossible. Cold water is the only thought you can hold in your mind; practice over, you drink so much you can't eat dinner. The thing that is carrying me through the week is the anticipation of a cold brew this upcoming Saturday night. The survival key for this phase of camp (conditioning) is entirely mental—if you start to hurt, think of other things and keep plodding.

Felt pretty good rolling out of the sack this morning, no stiffness, a little bounce in my legs; I had a good morning practice, but this afternoon it all came back. Dead tired again, but tomorrow . . . always tomorrow. Tomorrow I'll feel better, tomorrow we play San Diego—not the real Chargers, but the rookies down at Irvine. There are three other NFL teams training in southern California besides the Cowboys, so it appears we will fill our weeks scrumming with their rookies until our veterans come on to camp. This San Diego game marks the opening of the 1970 season, with a potential slate of thirty games before it's all over. Thirty games?

Two guys left for home this morning, both offensive linemen. They make the third and fourth to leave on their own. One of them was my suite-mate next door, a big, free-agent tackle from Cincinnati. The trainers had been around that morning to inform some of the heavier players they would have to lose weight. My neighbor was faced with losing fifteen pounds in seven days, so he left. The other man to leave was Jerry Dossey, an eighth-round pick from Arkansas; not the quitting type I thought. During rookie orientation we were out in sweat clothes and it was Jim Myers' bright idea to hold a pass-rush drill "just to see some movement." We lined up one-on-one and started the drill. On the first play Doug Mooers faked Dossey and had him beat; Dossey dove for Mooers' legs and cut him down. Anybody who cares enough to cut in a purely movement drill has to be a real competitor. Anyway, Dossey is gone, and he was probably the best offensive lineman in camp. I think his problem was that he was never told he was doing well; he became depressed at his lack of progress and went home. Dossey reinforces my theory that if you concentrate on the crap, the humiliations, and the aches, you can kiss yourself good-bye.

We were discussing motivation tonight, and most of the group were of the opinion that financial rewards are incentive enough. To some of us, however, the financial end appears not exactly secure, so why subject yourself?

Cliff felt there was more to it than money. He sensed an

intangible something lurking out there waiting to be grasped.

"Football is an opportunity," he said. "It's a chance to do something you enjoy, to be paid for doing it . . . and . . . to become somebody."

I stumble on the subject.

Before every practice Pete Athas, a brash cornerback out of the Continental League, methodically checks into the training room and announces some kind of injury. Today his knee was bothering him.

"Here," Pete said, rubbing the inside of his right knee. "It really hurts."

Trainer Larry Gardner strolled over to have a look. He bent down and exerted pressure on the inside of the joint. "Does that hurt?" he asked.

"Yes," Pete said.

"Could be serious."

Gardner looked concerned. He pushed a table out of the way, and cleared some floor space. "Get down on all fours," Larry instructed.

Athas got down on his hands and knees.

"Now," Larry said, "can you lift up your right leg without extending your knee?"

Athas carefully lifted his right leg.

"A little bit higher," Larry said. "It doesn't hurt, does it?"

"Well . . . no," Athas said, and hoisted his right leg as high as it would go.

"Now bark," Gardner said, and walked out of the room.

Time seems to be frozen.

Yesterday came the first major cut outside of physicals. Those disappearing included Leon Coleman (an Olympic hurdler), Walter Hawkins (a basketball player), and Laurence Jarmon (a fat man). Eight in all; most notable was my friend Neal Smith. Coleman and Hawkins did not develop the feel and temperament required (they had an entire week), but I had thought Neal would be around for a while. Gil Brandt claimed he was just too slow.

Neal's situation is an ironic one. Competitiveness is supposed to be an essential ingredient in a professional athlete; Neal is competitive to a fault. Besides, in the twelve-minute test he ran farther than any of the other eighty people. I can't figure it. They didn't even let him scrimmage today. On the opposite end of the spectrum is Larry Jarmon, 6 feet 8 inches and close to 300 pounds. Larry lagged about fifteen minutes behind in all events and, true to form, turned a little over a quarter mile in the twelve-minute test. It's a shame that Neal had to go out on the same plane with him.

Walter Hawkins and I had played basketball against each other quite frequently back in high school in northern Virginia. Gil told me the Hawk had been an aggressive college basketball player at the University of Utah and deserved a shot at football. Gil found Walter earlier this summer working in the kitchen of a Hot Shoppes restaurant in suburban Virginia. He took him outside and timed Hawk in a forty-yard dash. Walter ran in his loafers . . . on the sidewalk . . . and turned a 4.6. Gil gave him a thousand dollars.

We won the scrimmage against San Diego. It wasn't very exciting, particularly after I realized that the guy across from me was just a free agent from nowhere trying to do the impossible. I was prepared for Lance Alworth and John Hadl; I couldn't adjust to Kermit Woodfolk from Harvey Mudd U.

Cliff and I noticed at the scrimmage that the trainers were testing various quick-energy drinks on us. Today's favorite was a raspberry-pineapple Sportade combination that left a pink film over teeth, gums, and tongue. These quick-energy specials are made to get into your system fast, and this one certainly did. In addition to pink-mouth, the side effects included all phases of Montezuma's revenge.

Anyway, it was Saturday night and time to relax. John Fitzgerald, Denton Fox (from Texas Tech; we had met at the Blue–Gray game), and I made the two-mile drive into Thousand Oaks, stopped at a bowling alley, and fired down beer until midnight. Then home to bed, tired but refreshed by the change of pace.

A new week and an early surprise. In the team meeting tonight good old Coach Myers inadvertently told his offensive linemen that probably none of them would make the club. Needless to say that touched off a minor furor and created a terrific attitude for practice tomorrow. It is evident that they are postponing a major cut until the veterans come in, and I am wondering now if all the rookies are in the same boat as the offensive linemen.

This morning I wasn't worth a damn in practice. I couldn't get past thinking how nice it would be to find myself on the next plane out of here. Things are at least settling into a routine now; you can count on Coach Myers to say something encouraging every day. When the veterans come in, there will surely be a major upheaval; we are getting too comfortable and most of us must go.

There is a man here who has been offering me unsolicited encouragement—keep hustling, etc. For a long time I wondered who in the hell he was, and today he refreshed my memory. He is an older man and a scout. He timed me in a forty-yard dash at school last fall and filed a good recommendation with the Cowboys (he claims). I think what happens is that if I do well, then he does well also in the way of a nice bonus. It's great to know someone is pulling for you.

Tomorrow there's another San Diego scrimmage, and everybody's ass is dragging. The coaches seem bored with their stumbling rookies and I don't blame them, but the feeling is spreading to the players.

The number of rookies has thinned out, so we have reshuffled roommates. I am now upstairs with Fitz, in an area better known as Marlboro Country. Denton and Fitz don't eat, just smoke; there are cigaret butts all over the place.

Something unusual happened in practice today. It involved Reggie Rucker, a black split receiver off last year's taxi squad,* Pete Athas, and Cliff. A pass-coverage drill was in process and Reggie got into a hassle with Cliff. Cliff won't admit it, but he is sparkling in practice. He hits with an uncivilized vengeance and our receivers don't like it. On this particular play Harris smashed Rucker just as the ball arrived, and Reggie missed the pass. Reggie took a few wild swings at Cliff and they both retreated to their respective huddles; a typical on-the-field jostle. After practice Athas was talking to Margene Adkins and stated that if Cliff had been black, nothing would have happened. Adkins relayed the comment to Reggie and Reggie stormed back, "YOU GOT ANY SHIT FOR ME?!" Athas stood up and started to stutter through an explanation when . . . POOM! *snap* . . . a broken jaw for Athas and six weeks out.

Yesterday we scrimmaged the 49er rookies. Played my usual so-so. We lost on the last play of the game when our quarterback pitched out to one of their defensive linemen. At this point I am naturally more concerned with how *I* play than with how we do as a team; Tom Landry's final judgment of my ability will be based on my performance in these rookie scrums and the upcoming exhibition games. Whether the team wins or loses is inconsequential—if I do not play well . . . I've lost.

---

* An NFL football team consists of forty active players, who dress out for all games, and seven inactive players, who do not dress out for games. These seven players comprise the taxi squad, so called because at one time its members drove cabs to supplement their incomes, which are substantially less than those of the active players.

Saturday night . . . a night out. As usual Fox, Cliff and I rushed down to the local hang-out in the bowling alley (the Po-Po Room) and downed some beer. Our evenings out are losing their effectiveness. At 6:30 on any given Wednesday or Saturday night all the rookies line up outside the dorm for the bus-for-town. We get off the bus at the same empty bar, stare at each other for four hours, then queue up again, drunk, for the ride back. I'm getting tired of looking at these guys and they're getting tired of looking at me, but there is no escape.

My brother spent the night, and this morning we fled to San Clemente and the beach. Out and gone, complete relaxation. Found upon my return that we would go to one practice a day until the veterans arrive (hooray!). Also, a two-dollar-a-day raise is in order. Tremendous. That jumps us up to twelve dollars for every day we put in—amazingly low for such specialized labor.

Wednesday we will have another game with the 49ers. They certainly keep the pressure on us to perform. The exhibition season is getting perilously close, and still no veterans. What will they do with us? Send us home? Cut the entire lot? Play the season with us? I wanna go home.

Yesterday we each received our playbook—a tome full of nomenclature, costing the individual five hundred dollars if it is lost. In the introductory section is a list of the rookies who signed to come to camp. Seventy-five names are there; only thirty-six people are left. Among these thirty-six are several guys who keep things pretty loose; Rick Shaw is one. Rick is big and blond, down from the Canadian League, where he was All-Pro. Training camps are nothing new to him. One night last week, bored and bedraggled, we settled into our room for a serious evening of doing nothing. There was a light tap on the door. Cliff lethargically reached over from the bed and flipped it open. Shaw was leaning against the doorpost, right hand on his hip, clad only in a Cowboy T-shirt, and an erection.

"Hi guys," he lisped, and strutted down the hall to the next room. We roared.

Rick Johnson also keeps things fairly loose. Rick is an offensive lineman from a small church school in Oregon; an ardent fisherman, his favorite pastime is trolling Alaskan shores. Klondike Johnson has fantasized the entire training-camp operation as a Walt Disney enterprise, with his coach, Jim Myers, playing the role of Uncle Walt himself. Uncle Walt and Klondike don't get on too well. When Myers informed the fellows that none of them would make the team, Klondike raised his hand and demanded his passage home . . . immediately.

"If none of us is going to make the team," he said, "why in hell did you invite me into this pit?"

Specialized labor at only twelve dollars per day.

Today the one-a-day practices began, and at last I have some time to myself. It is Monday afternoon of the third week.

Last night we watched films of the San Francisco scrimmage. A linebacker named Butch Van Leuwan, from San Diego State, made some nice plays; he had several good licks, intercepted a pass, and recovered a fumble. Coach Landry's comment on his performance was favorable; "This is the kind of play we need to win football games," Tom said. Came the dawn, Van Leuwan was on his way back to San Diego. Others among the departed were Dunn, Brown, Kemp, and Blackburn.

I went down to get taped this morning and stumbled over a heap of discarded equipment: beat-up helmets, one with "Kemp" penned across the front, shoulder pads, worn-out pants . . . a pile of wasted dreams.

I've rationalized getting cut. It's no disgrace as long as you take your best shot.

Thursday. Downslide of the third week. We scrimmaged San Francisco again yesterday and smoked them 31–3.

Last night was the regular Wednesday night off and it was purely pitiful. Same empty bar, same beer, same bullshit. I left the bar about ten, read for an hour and slept.

Woke up to a sizable cut. Seven more. They cut Klondike Johnson, one of the better offensive linemen. A group of us were sitting around discussing the cut when Klondike came in with news of his release. Strangely, the personal relationships which had been cultivated over the weeks shifted. Klondike was on the outside now, and nobody knew what to say. One of the other offensive linemen, a guy named Edwards, offered the standard "Boy, I wish I were cut." We offered to kick his ass out of our room. Klondike went back to roving the Alaskan frontier.

Dissatisfaction is creeping through the ranks. The word going around is that the cuts have been lighter this year than in previous years because of the prolonged players' strike. After all, you've got to have players if you want to hold practice. The situation is becoming pretty obvious and there has been a parade of people down to see Coach Landry about getting the hell out. The only reason they have even stopped to see him is that an official release is needed, or all bonuses must be relinquished. It has gotten to such a point that after the last scrimmage Ernie Broadbeck, a tackle from the Ivy League, confronted Coach Landry with the facts of his situation: "Coach, I know you are only detaining me so there will be enough bodies for you to scrimmage. I've got better things to do with my time." T. L. hadn't been too receptive to the many similar requests, but he gave Ernie his walking papers.

In the wake of all these attitude problems, Tom dug deep into his bag of inspirational tricks. At the meeting last night he showed up with a cassette tape player slung over his shoulder and a tape in his hand. He instructed us to listen carefully. Earl Nightengale was the featured speaker, and his story was entitled "Acres of Diamonds." I must admit that I did not grow up listening to Mr. Nightengale, and I was therefore very interested in the reasons for his visit. With his first words the impact of his message was evident; Earl has one of those mellow, resonant baritones that cast a spell of instant slumber.

"Acres of Diamonds" is the story of a South African farmer who sold his farm to search for diamonds, only to find many years later that the diamonds he had been searching for had been right there on his own farm. After relating the sad tale of the South African farmer, Earl went into a twenty-minute dissertation on the hidden meanings of the story. Tom then applied the different themes of the story to the world of football in a twenty-minute dissertation of his own. It was all very effective. Only five people requested their release this morning.

Things are getting pretty messy with the players' strike. Some of the teams which didn't bring a lot of rookies to camp are closing their training facilities. If the Cowboys close down, I suspect we are all in trouble. I think they may have to pay us according to our contracts, but I'm not sure. At any rate the suspense thickens, and I wish it were September.

Cliff is spending all of his spare time in the company of his newly acquired playbook. It is impossible to drag him away from his desk, even on our free evenings. On the other hand, Denton Fox is gradually going crazy in this dormitory. He fancies the night life and apparently the bed check is weighing heavily. I look for Fox to get nabbed in a curfew violation pretty soon—in fact, he was nearly caught last night. Denton went downtown and didn't come back until after midnight. Dan Reeves had already been around checking. . . . It could have been costly, but Reeves gave him a break.

The afternoons drip on by. The veterans are still on strike and the end is not in sight. We hum along. Scrim-

mage the Ram rookies tomorrow; that will total five games
in two weeks. It gets harder and harder to get mentally
ready to play. Against San Francisco I didn't really get
going until the second half; I am thirsty for some *real*
games.

The room is starting to fill with fellow wall watchers. My
partner from Vanderbilt, Bob Asher, is in Chicago for the
College All-Star game. They play Kansas City tonight and
he'll probably get here Sunday or Monday. He has written
several letters, saying nothing, mostly apprehensive about
camp. He has a right to be a little scared; that All-Star
game doesn't do a thing for your chances of making an
NFL team, particularly if you get hurt.

Fox and Fitz are now into a rousing game of Fish. We've
exhausted everything else.

August at last! The end of a funny weekend and the
beginning of the fourth week.

In camp with us is a little guy from Zambia, Africa—
twenty-six years old, cherubic sort of face, very proper English. His name is Howard Ma-ku-ta, and he is a placekicker of unusual talent. The other day when he was out
kicking forty-yard shots he pulled a muscle in his right leg.
Coach Stautner told him to go in and see the trainer for
treatment. Howard said no, motioned the holder to change
sides, and promptly started kicking left-footed!

In addition to his kicking duties, Howard has taken over
the week-night, premeeting festivities. He has insisted
that we learn an African tribal chant; Howard sings something in his native tongue and the group chants back the
chorus: *"San-sa-kur."* It builds. . . . Howard goes into this
dance. . . .

Yesterday before the Ram scrum we were all sitting
around the locker room, dressed and ready to go. The Ram
players were late, wandering around, getting taped, and

going through other pregame necessities. Howard stood up in the midst of all this and started thumping on his Riddell helmet, *whap . . . whap.* We picked it up, and after a ten-minute fertility dance Howard eased into his crescendo-chant. The Ram players were puzzled, skittery: "What in the hell? . . . What is this weeeird shit? Voodoo." Right. They were scared, we were psyched, . . . and we rolled.

After supper we went down to the bowling alley and annihilated ourselves on beer.

Bob ("Smasher") Asher, Charlie Waters, and Duane Thomas flew in yesterday from the College All-Star game in Chicago. Asher is even bigger than I remembered. When we were at Vanderbilt the pro scouts passing through fell passionately in love with Bob. They driveled all over him: "You're a number-one draft pick, Bob. GODDAMMIT! YOU'RE A NUMBER ONE!" The scouts' advances to me were of the "no chance" variety: "Son," they said politely, "your legs are awfully skinny. . . ." I didn't really pay much attention; I was having too much fun needling Asher, Vanderbilt's resident hero. Bob was All-City, All-State, All-Conference, All-American; a participant in the North–South Shrine game, the American Bowl, the Senior Bowl; and inevitably a top draft choice in the annual NFL draft.

"Asher," I lectured, "you're going to be a meathead your entire life."

Bob was drafted in the second round by the Cowboys, I went in the sixth, . . . and here we are; Saturday night . . . Thousand Oaks, California, . . . the Po-Po Room . . . one meathead getting drunk, the other watching.

Tom introduced the new arrivals at tonight's meeting, and we were off on another week's adventure. Of the three new people, Charlie Waters faces the most difficult path to fame and fortune. Duane Thomas and Smasher Asher were number-one and number-two draft choices respectively; traditionally this virtually assures them a position somewhere on the squad come September. From the third round on down, however, there are no more sure things. Charlie, one of three third-round selections (along with Steve Kiner and Denton Fox), is further hampered by the fact that he is a quarterback/receiver trying to make the switch to defensive back. He has already missed three crucial weeks of practice.

Charlie came out of his first meeting, chin to chest, completely overwhelmed. Cliff jerked him back into the meeting room and set logically about to bring him up to date. I should hasten to add that this is not exactly recommended behavior. Helping someone who might take your spot on the club is obviously self-defeating, but Cliff and Charlie had become friends during the rookie orientation weekend in February, and friends are to be helped.

Charlie is instantly likable. He has a quick, dimpled grin that easily expands to an engaging laugh. A slow Carolina drawl enhances his considerable good looks; his face is narrow, well scrubbed, and framed by a thick mane of hair and a long, slender neck; his eyes are sleepy and brown. Charlie stands 6 feet 2 inches tall and weighs approximately 200 pounds; he is not as fast or as mesomorphic as Cliff, but just as scrappy.

Cliff explained to him the rudiments of all the pass defenses and Charlie carefully copied down the pertinent points.

"This is a lot of shit to remember," Cliff remarked.

"No problem," Charlie said. "I'm going to copy it all down on some adhesive tape and tape it to my wrist. When the defenses are called, I'll check my cheat-sheet and know exactly what to do."

Charlie came out to practice this afternoon, wrists taped and ready. He overlooked one small consideration, however—sweat. Adhesive tape does not stick to a wet surface very long, and twenty minutes into practice Charlie lost his new-found knowledge.

"Back to the drawing board," Charlie said, but there may not be enough time. The veterans are coming in.

All hell is breaking loose. The imminent arrival of the veterans sends a shiver; we have been around here for some time and grown accustomed to training-camp life; the veterans seem to be imposing on us, whereas we are the actual imposers. Adjustment time.

Another big cut this morning. The dirty deed is done over the telephone. On the morning of a cut the phones start ringing in sequence according to the room numbers of the selected many. Generally I stay in bed listening until the ringing has passed our room and I'm sure I won't have to pack up. This morning our phone rang five times. Each time it was Coach Myers. Each time he was after someone else. On his fifth call, Fitz asked him to please call the operator for any further information.

One of the cuttees was Denton Fox. It was a shock to me, but especially to him: an All-American, third-round draft pick, with a twenty-thousand-dollar bonus. It was very awkward to say good-bye.

Today was the first full day with the vets, and what a day. The schedule was the worst of any we have had so far. I think we totaled not quite two hours to ourselves the entire day and night.

I was a bit anxious this morning, being in the presence of some of these guys; I felt like the Mayor of Tupelo at a United Nations function. All the players are well-known boyhood idols, and I'm wondering, again, what I am doing here.

The first veteran I got a look at was Walt Garrison, and the size thing struck me down once more. At 6 feet and

212 pounds, he was much too small to be Walt Garrison. I asked one of our trainers, Don Cochren, about Walt. "Yeah," Don said, "a lot of people make that assumption." He told me about the time a fan approached Garrison with that same thought on a road trip.

"Hey," the guy said, "you're too small to be a professional football player."

Walt looked up into his face. The fellow was about 6 feet 3.

"Want to try me?" Walt asked, and that took care of that.

The practice tempo for the remainder of camp was set today in our first full workout. Calvin Hill, the big fullback from Yale (235 pounds), accidentally ran over Lee Roy Jordan (215 pounds) and put him literally on his butt. This was during a dummy drill. I thought it was all over when Lee Roy picked himself up and things proceeded normally. In the last drill of the day, the team polish segment, Calvin ripped through the line like a crazed buffalo and ran smack into Lee Roy's well-placed forearm. Calvin went down hard. He contemplated retaliation for a moment, thought better of it, and returned to the huddle. There are subtle undercurrents flowing on this team, but at this rate nothing will be secret very long.

Tonight I had my shot at singing for my supper. It is traditional in NFL training camps for rookies to sing; you are required to put your hand over your heart, state your name and alma mater, and then sing the school fight song. Somehow Vanderbilt's fight song lacks . . . spunk:

> Dynamite, dynamite, when Vandy starts to fight,
> Down the field with blood to yield
> We'll win this game tonight.   *Rah. Rah. Rah.*

Kiner has had to put up with a lot of flack during his singing exploits because of a comment he made about Chuck Howley prior to camp. He delicately stated that he thought Howley was an old man, over the hill, and that he, Steve Kiner, was ready to step in and take over. Last night Kiner was singing "Happy Birthday" to Chuck.

Yesterday Lance Rentzel pulled in with his wife, Joey Heatherton. It was my first in-person study of a genuine, bona fide movie star. She was acting silly, wishing her "Dimples" good luck on the gridiron, but looking very nice all the same. I didn't actually meet her; Charlie, Cliff, and I were hiding in some nearby bushes, trying to be inconspicuous.

We were involved in a blitzing drill today and I somehow got mixed in with a veteran group. The offense lined up on the ball, and Chuck Howley, the linebacker on my side, gave me a "bullet" call. I had never heard of a bullet call. The ball snapped, and I took two steps upfield and stopped; Howley ran up my back.

"Uh, what do I do . . . ?"

"I don't care what the fuck you do," he said sharply, "just stay out of my way."

"Yes sir," I said.

Aaaah. After several beers in the dorm I am ready for anything (bed). Tonight's entertainment consisted of five of us cutting cards for a position on the team, low man out each time. I won. I will inform Coach Landry of my new status tomorrow.

Busy times. About like yesterday, only longer meetings and longer practices. Learned this morning that Denton Fox was claimed by three teams and will be initially heading for Chicago and the Bears. I hope he latches on up there, or somewhere; as he often said himself, the only skill he knows is football, and somehow there isn't much demand on the outside for a used jock. After five years in school he still lacked thirty-five hours for a degree. Unfortunately, guys like Denton are closer to the rule than the exception.

Yesterday in practice we were going through the usual pass-rush drill when Doug Mooers (rookie) accidentally beat Ralph Neely (All-Pro) several times in succession. Ralph demanded another go. He grabbed Mooers by the face mask, threw him to the ground, and proceeded to kick him vigorously in the ribs. That incident jolted most of us from our positions of reverent awe. I anticipate a more hostile attitude toward the veterans from now on.

It looks like I'm in pretty good shape in my battle for a position. Larry Cole and Willie Townes are the only two veteran defensive ends in camp, and the exhibition season is closing fast.

Saturday. Game tonight at eight in San Diego. A real game. We're leaving at noon.

Opportunity is rapping on my door. George Andrie, the starting right defensive end, has retired. This leaves only the two experienced ends I mentioned; I'm playing behind Townes. Because of an injury Fat Willie hasn't played in several years, and as a result he is having a hard time. The pressure falls on me; if I come along, I could start; if not, I could just as easily be gone.

To handle our dinner singing exploits with a minimum of embarrassment, we have formed a quartet: Charlie and I sing lead, Cliff and Fitz sing backup. We have entrusted Charlie, a Clemson graduate with a degree in Parks, Recreation, and Parties, with the selection and arrangement of material. Last night the television cameras for a sports broadcast were on us, and we came off pretty well. Our tune was Charlie's version of "Swinging on a Star":

> Would you like to swing on a star,   *da da da*
> Carry moonbeams home in a jar,   *da da da*
> And be better off than you are?   *da da da*
> Or would you rather be a rook? *

Well . . . it seemed like a good idea at the time.

---

* "Swinging on a Star" by Johnny Burke and James Van Heusen, © copyright 1944 Burke & Van Heusen, Inc. Copyright renewed. Copyright assigned to Bourne Co. and Dorsey Bros. Music Inc. Used by permission.

The game last night was a strange and revealing experience. I did all right, but I won't know until we see the films if I did any better than Willie Townes. Down in San Diego it struck me for the first time that the older veterans are beat to hell. After two days of practice Malcolm Walker could not get out of bed, much less walk. His knees are a mass of scar tissue and fluid, literally mangled. Some of the other guys have pulled muscles, ripped tendons, sore backs, are just physically beat-up. The training room before the game was an eerie place: cortisone, codeine, needles everywhere—all to numb the pain. Repeated at half time. I don't know. . . . Last night was the first time I ever felt like a contemporary gladiator. The field at San Diego has been scooped out of the ground, a ten-foot wall separates the lowest end-zone seats from the playing surface—down in the proverbial pit. I didn't get into the game until two minutes before the half, but I played most of the second half. After the first contact it was just another football game. Well, almost. It was all oddly cold. In the pregame locker room the veterans exchanged the standard "Have a good one," but there was a definite lack of sincerity . . . no esprit. Once the game began, each veteran player became solely concerned with his own particular job; the rookies were desperate to attract attention.

One of my colleagues was especially anxious to make a favorable impression. Bill Cornman is a smallish, red-headed, iron-handed receiver who led the universe in punt returns his senior year at University of the Pacific. Coach Landry kept him around through training camp to see if Bill could return a kick under game duress; the San Diego game provided his opportunity. He ran the first kick back for one yard and lost yardage on the second. After his second attempt Cornman came off the field dejected. "I'm not doing very well, am I?" he said. The third kick was heading for the safety, but goddammit Cornman hung in there; at the final second Bill leaped high in the air to execute a play seldom seen in modern football—the intercepted punt. He fumbled. Somehow Cornman came up with the ball in the ensuing scramble; he jumped to his

feet, held the ball high over his head as if he had just
scored a midfield touchdown, and looked to the bench for
approval. Coach Landry turned away . . . embarrassed.
Cornman was on the next bus home.

Monday. The last week of two-a-day practices. I woke
up this morning with that now familiar feeling of wanting
not to move . . . just to roll over and slip back to sleep; all
the physical contact is doing me in.

I discovered in my formative years of football that I was
not what you call your ferocious hitter. As a matter of fact,
I hated to hit, so I became a quarterback. That was in high
school. When I was a freshman in college the coaches uncovered two serious deficiencies in my quarterbacking talents: (1) I could not throw the deep pass very well, and (2)
I could not throw the short pass at all.

"Dad-jim, son," the coach said, "you're a fine student-
athlete, and you're going to make us a real fine defensive
end!"

I closed my eyes and eventually learned to hit, but to
this day it is not one of my favorite pastimes.

"I was a pussy too," Charlie Waters admitted in an after-
dinner discussion of hitting. "All through college I was
one of the glory guys, quarterback . . . wide receiver, but
the Cowboy computer said 'backpedal,' and shit, here I
am on defense."

Charlie is undergoing the same changes I suffered
through as a freshman in college, and he is experiencing
the same results. He delivered his first professional lick in
the San Diego game, and he's still carrying the accompanying effect—a splitting headache.

Cliff, out of necessity, is the most adept at the business
of hitting.

"I've got no choice," he said. "At my size I've got to
have a perfect angle and a full head of steam to bring anybody down; I just can't tackle a two-hundred-and-thirty-
pound fullback straight on more than one time . . . no

way! I suppose it's just an aggressive tendency . . . little guys need it to get by; big guys don't. . . .

"Let me explain it this way," Cliff continued. "I've been having this dream out here; I'm standing on a highway and this guy is coming at me on a motorcycle. Now what would you do in that situation?"

"What any sane person would do," I said. "Hit the ditch."

"Okay, but I don't hit the ditch. I break down and smash the guy with a forearm as he goes by."

A cut was scheduled for this morning and it came as expected. Five more players were eliminated—the most notable, Rick Shaw. To me Shaw represented a slice of . . . the life: All-Pro in Canada, a new Cadillac Eldorado, expensive clothes, a fine-looking wife, entirely irresponsible. I thought he played well Saturday night, so did he. Too bad.

This morning's practice was very difficult. Stautner worked us like dogs on that two-man sled, having us push it and push it until all legs refused to function. I think he did this for George Andrie's sake. George came back from retirement yesterday. Enough. One more practice and the day is over.

It is traditional in Thousand Oaks for the rookies to wait on the veterans to a limited extent. The main chore is retrieving ice from the cafeteria and carrying it to one of the vets' rooms to ice down their beer. It seems that everyone has a cooler and everyone has a post-practice beer or two. I asked Bob Lilly if this has been a custom down through the years; he said that it was the only way he knew to maintain sanity during training camp.

Coach Landry had some choice comments about the situation before tonight's meeting. He stated that since we were quartered in a Lutheran school we ought to refrain from drinking in our rooms . . . out of due respect. "What if the league office found out about this?" he asked. "I must be naïve, but I can't imagine this kind of thing going on." Hmmmm. Players have been enjoying post-practice beer for ten years, and Tom has just now found out about it.

Coach Landry is pressing to beat the Rams: "This is the kind of team we must whip to get to the Super Bowl" is the credo this week. The pressure seeps directly to the players. Last night Charlie, Cliff, and I chipped in, bought a case of beer, and iced it down before the evening meeting. When the meeting adjourned we were ready for some serious beer drinking. After two beers Charlie noted that Cliff had disappeared. We found him downstairs . . . watching a Ram game film. It was 10:30 P.M.

Cliff admitted to being hooked by Coach Landry's analysis, but the clincher was in a copy of the Los Angeles *Times* Cliff had stuffed in his hip pocket. An article in the sports section carried a list of the player match-ups for our upcoming game with the Rams:

Bob Lilly——Tom Mack
George Andrie——Charlie Cowan
. . . .
Cliff Harris——Roman Gabriel

"That's me," Cliff said, pointing emphatically at the article. "Cliff Harris versus Roman Gabriel . . . man . . . I can't believe it! Me and Roman Gabriel. I've got to get ready!"

Tomorrow night we present the much-heralded rookie show. It is made up of sarcastic little bitter-skits aimed at ripping the hell out of everyone. It is our only good shot at some of the asses on this team. We enjoy something akin to congressional immunity in that we can say anything about anybody in the organization and not be (severely) penalized. It must be kept clean, however. Danny Reeves delivered the introductory monologue for the 1965 edition of the show from a classic, "full moon" position: butt to the audience, hands clasped to the ankles . . . and no clothes. Mrs. Landry and Mrs. Schramm were not impressed.

Wallowing in the depths, swallowing my integrity. I am at the mercy of . . . Ernie Stautner? How did I come to this? My progress is a mystery. I have no idea how I am doing and no one in power will give me so much as a hint. There is another cut on Monday, so I won't be kept in suspense too long. It seems this restless, dissatisfied feeling permeates the team; everyone is on edge. The coaches bitch at the players, the players bitch at each other.

The rookie show had its high spots. I was surprised at the cast's proficiency in front of a discerning audience; some of the coaches, however, took the humor in a serious vein. The critics' acclaim went to Bob Asher for his portrayal of Jim Myers' nose. Coach Myers has a broad, shattered snoz and Asher played him with his nose plastered flat against his face with adhesive tape. Myers hasn't spoken to Bob since.

When you are worn out, beaten down physically, and mentally unsure of your status, you come to doubt yourself and the inner resources you came with. These two-a-days are Chinese torture in that respect. We've set some kind of record at this point with four weeks' worth.

We play the Rams tomorrow night. The post-game itinerary calls for us to spend the night in a motel near the airport and get an early-morning flight into Dallas. Thousand Oaks is becoming a little hard to take.

Back in Dallas. We are quartered here in the lovely Holiday Inn Central. The lobby and rooms have been decorated in a nauseating lavender and hot-pink motif, and there are large Dmitri Vail portraits covering every available inch of wall space. Dmitri, whoever he is, has a permanently reserved table in the dining room. The food tastes like my closet.

Charlie and Cliff are quartered down the hall and we have established a routine to handle the unbelievable schedule. I had thought training camp was harsh. We were informed early this week that two-a-days would continue. The rookie bus departs each morning at dawn, and delivers us safely back to the Inn by 6:00 P.M.

"The only thing we can do about this," Charlie said, "is get drunk."

The Ram game was sloppy. We lost it in one of those ho-hum contests that seem to characterize exhibition games. The gladiator feeling really grabs at you in the L. A. Coliseum; walking down that long tunnel . . . bursting into the arena; people in the cheap seats shouting, booing; then the game, like San Diego, just another game. Somehow no one seems to give a damn.

Dave Whitsell was an exception. He is a small, aging defensive back who came to camp after being released by the New Orleans Saints. He had had some good days with the Chicago Bears, but he lost a crucial step of speed and was cut; he drifted to New Orleans, then Dallas. Whitsell was a ball of fire in Thousand Oaks. He cornered Charlie Waters on several occasions and asked him when the rookies would be cleared out so the big boys could get down to business. I guess he hoped that with all the noise he was making his lack of speed would go unnoticed. It didn't. Dave's fate was sealed the first day back in Dallas. It is said that Whitsell was stationed at a urinal in the men's room up in the Cowboy offices when Tom came in and assumed a stance at the adjacent urinal. Whitsell looked up.

"Tom," he asked, "how long have you been bald?"
Good-bye Dave Whitsell.

I was notified several days ago to appear for my draft physical, and as I think about it, the situation takes on a new, more crucial aspect. If I am to be cut, Gil will not waste his resources on releasing me from the grasp of Uncle Sam. Instead, he will let me pass the physical and proceed directly to basic training. What a shock that would be. I hope Gil has as much influence as he seems to have.

I proceeded down to the examining center, where I was:

> injected
> inspected
> detected
> infected
> neglected
> and
> see-lected (almost).*

I had high blood pressure. If I have it for three days straight, I'm out.

I didn't have high blood pressure, but I did have enough bone chips floating around in my knee to qualify for disqualification.

Tomorrow we meet the Green Bay Packers.

Game days, particularly during the exhibition season (games are scheduled at night), tend to become very long and thin. As in college, the players generally lie around in their hotel rooms and watch television, but here there is

* "Alice's Restaurant" by Arlo Guthrie, © copyright 1966, 1967 by Appleseed Music Inc. All rights reserved. Used by permission.

an added bonus for movie freaks. Walt Garrison is in charge of selecting movies for the team to watch to help kill the afternoon. This morning the movie was *The Cincinnati Kid*, this afternoon, *The Hustler*. I hope Paul Newman can give us enough lift to get by Green Bay. If we lose, two-a-days will continue, and I'll have to quit.

We lost to Green Bay 35–34. I didn't play too much. Six plays. But on two of them I got to the great (old) Bart Starr before he could dump the ball. . . . A thrill, a flash, but then back to the bench.

There is a big cut due Monday, the biggest yet; sixteen guys must leave for the club to get down to the required forty-seven (forty on the active squad and seven on the taxi squad). I think I may be one of the select this trip; I haven't played much in the exhibition season, and Ernie hasn't spoken to me in some time. Cut . . . the only good aspect of going now is the release of all pressure, total relaxation. The problems revolve around the fact that it is now too late to enroll in school, so I'm assured a position in the armed forces—the last place I want to spend the next two years.

The ritual of the cut here at the Holiday Inn is a little different than it was in Thousand Oaks. Most of the players eat breakfast and lunch in the Inn restaurant. It becomes impossible to reach the lucky player in his room, so he is paged in the dining area: "Otto Brown, please see Coach Landry in Room 219." All the others stare into their plate . . . the ultimate humiliation. The night before each cut takes place, Charlie, Cliff, and I meet behind locked doors and trim the roster ourselves. Surprisingly enough, we have been right a good percentage of the time, but as the deadline draws nearer, our selections get tougher to make. We met one night last week to pick out six likely candidates for the next day's cut; we trimmed five guys without much trouble, but still had to come up with one more. We pored over the roster for twenty minutes without much success. Finally Cliff and I looked at each other . . . and we cut Charlie. It was all in good fun ("Ha-ha," Charlie said) until Charlie got a call the next day from Coach Myers, instructing him to visit Coach Landry with his playbook. Charlie asked us all into his room. He had started to pack, and we were attempting those awkward good-byes when the phone rang again. It was Coach Myers, the man with the velvet touch, saying it had all been a big mistake.

Sunday. Day off. As a respite from the drudgery of the Holiday Inn routine, and to escape the escalating anxiety of Monday's final cut, Cliff and I journeyed down to a doctor friend's ranch. Our friend's name is John Knox and he owns fifteen hundred acres of pasture and pecan trees down south of Mexia, Texas.

When we arrived, Dr. Knox fetched two feisty cutting horses and we mounted up for a midmorning jaunt. My horse refused to leave the corral; Cliff, however, took off—a born equestrian.

"I didn't know Cliff could ride," Dr. Knox remarked.

"I didn't either," I said.

He couldn't. Cliff had lost control. His horse was headed for a barbed-wire fence at full throttle. At the last instant the animal veered into the low branches of a mesquite tree. A thick limb caught Cliff square in the chest and he did a beautiful half gainer, landing perfectly on his head.

Cliff was visibly shaken, but uninjured. Dr. Knox checked him, then offered his one-eyed mare in exchange for the cutting horse. Cliff politely refused, remounted, and disappeared. Dr. Knox and I adjourned to the house for iced tea.

An hour later Cliff trotted confidently up to the house. The horse was exhausted, sopped with perspiration, and drooling blood. "Whoa," Cliff said and the horse stopped immediately. Cliff, grinning, dismounted and asked if there was any more tea.

We spent the rest of the day hunting and fishing, and in all it was a great escape. With dusk came thoughts of tomorrow's final cut, and it became necessary to get back to Dallas . . . and brood.

The anxiety that started to build last night turned to frustration today. The six o'clock news reported that the Cowboys have cut ten people and will sign six others to the taxi squad, but the names won't be released until Wednesday.

Tuesday night. I'm suddenly looking pretty good in the battle for a position. This afternoon Coach Landry dealt away one of my competitors, Clarence Williams, to the Green Bay Packers.

"You a little happier today?" Dan Reeves asked me at practice.

I wasn't sure.

"There's another little surprise due later this week," he said.

I hope this is not Reeves' idea of a practical joke. My future has boiled down to twenty-four hours and the thinking of one man, Tom Landry. It's frightening. Tomorrow I could have everything . . . or practically nothing.

The cut. Friend Fitz is gone, possibly to the cab squad; the rest of the selected players seemed to disappear into the night. Everyone but Willie Townes; he left this morning and I was shoved right into his locker directly between Bob Lilly and Jethro Pugh and this is all very awkward, almost embarrassing. Nobody seems to notice it, but I have made this team!

2

TRIPTYCHS

Cliff Harris and Charlie Waters shared my ebullition; somehow we had all made it through and survived the final cut. The evening of our official emergence as Dallas Cowboys was spent in a drunken jig . . . bubbling around the Holiday Inn, a late-night, nude dip in the Inn pool. At 3:00 A.M. the self-congratulatory celebration ended; our ecstasy faded like a madras shirt. We had made the team, yes; but there were still meetings to attend, games to play—the season was not over, it was just beginning. It also occurred to us that we were frittering away our last free night in the motel; the following day the Cowboys would stop paying the rent and we would be out on the street. Charlie and I set about scavenging Holiday Inn towels, pillows, and *objets d'art* for the apartments we would have to rent.

Of the three of us, during training camp, Charlie and I had been at times (very) quietly confident we would end up with the club in some capacity, probably in the traditional role of the rookie: a ground-pounding-sacrificial-suicide-squad-berserk-o. We were right. Cliff, unsure of himself and his status most of the time, was named the starting free safety for the league opener with Philadelphia.

Cliff's reaction to the news was absolute shock, and the

daze lasted for five weeks. On Sundays, Cliff covered the field like a pinball, running constantly, hitting savagely, and never tiring. It seemed he was breathing pure oxygen. He was selected Most Valuable Player in three of the first five games. Coach Landry consistently singled Cliff out as a perfect example of hustle and determination. Between games Cliff found himself out on the town with such superstars as Lee Roy Jordan, or over to Walt Garrison's for barbecued ribs. His phone never stopped ringing. It was a dream.

The fifth weekend of the season we were up in Minneapolis to play the Vikings in a crucial game. I filed off the players' bus, bought a newspaper in the lobby of the hotel, and ambled up to my twelfth-floor room. The door was ajar, my roomie was already there. Cliff was glumly slumped over the radiator next to the window, casually dissecting a deck of Braniff playing cards and flipping them out the window. The airborne cards, caught in an updraft, were fluttering wildly outside the window.

"What is it, Cliff?" I asked carefully.

"Agh. The goddamn cards won't float down to the street."

"I don't mean that. . . . You look sick."

Cliff didn't answer, so I turned on the television. Chris Schenkel was analyzing some midwestern college game. He was on every channel.

"It's the army," Cliff said at length. "Gil is running into problems with the people in Washington."

"You're in the National Guard, right?"

"Yeah."

"Well, what in the hell is the problem?"

"Active duty."

"Shit, Cliff, the Cowboys can get them to postpone your duty for three months. The military people will understand what this means. Forget about it."

As we made our final approach into Dallas late Sunday night following the game, Coach Landry came back and asked Cliff to see him when we landed.

"How'd you play?"

"Shitty . . . but not that shitty."

Cliff waited until everyone disembarked before he searched out Coach Landry. Tom was standing in the deserted corridor with Tex Schramm and Gil Brandt. Tom spoke.

"Cliff, I've got bad news for you: you've got to report to Fort Polk, Louisiana by 6:30 A.M. tomorrow. Now, I know . . ."

Cliff took temporary leave of his senses. He unleashed a string of obscenities and began flailing wildly: he battered a trash can senseless, tipped over a gate marker, and threw his playbook twenty-five yards. Tom, Tex, and Gil disappeared. When Cliff got to the car, he was sobbing out of frustration.

"Goddamn, this has to happen, . . . and the Cowboys . . . they knew I'd have to go . . . they knew the whole fucking time."

Cliff attacked the dashboard.

We had lost to Minnesota 54–13.

With Cliff gone, Richmond Flowers was the heir apparent to the free-safety position. Richmond, a former world-class hurdler and wingback/receiver from the University of Tennessee, had not quite adjusted to the rigors of playing defense in the NFL. His methods were considered . . . unorthodox.

Following the Minnesota debacle we met the Kansas City Chiefs in Kansas City. Midway through the first half, a Kansas City player was streaking up the sidelines with the football. Richmond moved in for the kill. Instead of knocking the guy out of bounds, Richmond stepped out into the air in classic hurdler form, spun his extended leg into the shins of the oncoming ballplayer, and tripped him cleanly in front of our bench. Tom was flabbergasted. The play earned Richmond a fifteen-yard penalty, the nickname "Whirlybird," and a seat on the bench. Charlie Waters moved in for Richmond.

It was ironic that Charlie, the freshly appointed free

safety, was even on the field. Charlie had actually been cut
during the preseason: the episode with Jim Myers had not
been a mistake; they had, indeed, let him go. But an alert
coach had then discovered that since Charlie had been a
participant in the College All-Star game, a decision on him
was not due until the next week. Charlie was recalled.

The day after the mix-up, Tom assembled Charlie, Richmond, and Cliff for a head-to-head forty-yard dash. It
seemed that the results of the race would determine who
would go and who would stay. Charlie was a little concerned. In training camp he had turned a 4.7 in the sprint;
Cliff and Richmond were in the 4.5–4.6 category. On this
day they all ran 4.6's. Tom let it ride. The Houston game
was upcoming and someone would surely shine through.

Someone did. It was Jerry LeVias, the Oiler wide receiver. LeVias beat veteran defensive back Otto Brown
unmercifully. As a result Cliff, Richmond, and Charlie
were home free. Otto was called out of the Holiday Inn
noon buffet and sent to New York.

Charlie's addition to the starting lineup added a new
dimension to the streamlined image of a defensive back.
Charlie is a floppy guy—an excellent athlete, but floppy
(some of the young ladies around town liken him to a
cocker-spaniel puppy). He had a penchant for cumber-
some, black, Puma soccer shoes and a healthy psychological dependence on Stick-um, the pencil-colored goop that
receivers and defensive backs spread all over themselves
to help catch the football; Charlie didn't have much confidence in his hands. His white sweat socks lounged aes-
thetically around his ankles, and there was always a towel
haphazardly stuffed in his belt to cope with the Stick-um
and the sweat. Charlie looked as though he had spent his
life playing football in the mud.

Nevertheless, he took to his position well. He starred.
Although Charlie is not as aggressive as Cliff, he covered
the field in the same manner: he made the big plays.
Coach Landry began to single him out in meetings for his
hustle and dedication. Off the field, Charlie started show-

ing up in three-hundred-dollar suits; he found himself out
on the town with Danny Reeves . . . Walt Garrison. Charlie was to be the only rookie in the Cowboys' defensive
lineup for Super Bowl V. Soon after Cliff's departure,
Charlie achieved the status of veteran player, a Dallas
Cowboy.

Meanwhile, I spent my time waiting. In training camp I
had falsely assumed that a rookie's selection to the forty-
man squad meant immediate acceptance and credibility.
Such was not the case. Cliff and Charlie's meteoric rise to
respectability clearly showed that in order to become an
integral part of the team, one must play regularly, and play
well. I was covering kicks.

"Covering kicks" does not adequately describe my ad-
ventures on the bomb squads. At 6 feet 6 inches 250
pounds I was hard pressed to out-quick the linebackers
and other savages who populated our opponents' return
teams. I was getting slaughtered.

For the opening kickoff against Philadelphia in the first
league game, I found myself situated at midfield in the
number-five position—the . . . ahem . . . "wedge-
buster." I was nervous. Mike Clark kicked off and I started
my sprint for the wedge, but my feet felt as though they
were sticking in the synthetic turf. I had run a good fifteen
yards when I picked up a flash of green off to the right.
Too late. The flash of green knocked me on my head. A
coach's voice exploded from my subconscious: "GET UP!
GET UP!!!" I tried, but it was too late again. A flash of
green from the left side put me on my butt. The play was
over. The tackle was made on the nineteen-yard line; . . .
the chalk in my mouth tasted like the forty. The two Eagle
bastards laughed. I quickly tired of covering kicks.

Unfortunately, my options were limited. On Sundays I
continued to master the subtle nuances of the kicking
game (ha); during the week I could only prepare for the
games as if I were actually going to play. By midseason I

was bored. A rookie's role in practice is similar to that of the illustrious B-team player in college: fodder for the big boys. When our offense worked, I was out there trying to portray the various football personalities of defensive ends around the league: if we were playing the Vikings, I was Jim Marshall; for the Giants I was Fred Dryer. When the defensive drills rolled around, the starting players moved in, and the fellows who needed the work moved out—a vicious circle that could only be broken by injury.

As we approached the ninth game of the season—five wins, three losses, and headed down the tubes—the pressure to upgrade our collective performance reached several thousand psi. In a light scrimmage that week, defensive end Larry Cole forearmed tackle Ron East's helmet and was forced to visit the trainer. Larry Gardner quickly diagnosed the injury as a potential calcium buildup, taped the forearm, and urged Cole to rejoin the drill. Larry had a broken arm.

I was ready to step in . . . mentally, anyway. An obstacle, however, lay buried in the opportunity. The problem revolved around the fact that Cole was the left end and I was a right end; for a right-hander, playing left end is like shooting a left-handed hook in basketball. Ernie came to my rescue. For two days he treated me as his firstborn; he spent every conceivable minute tutoring me in technique, opponent's tendencies, etc., and I was suddenly ready.

The game was a Monday-night affair against the St. Louis Cardinals. Coach Landry joined the defensive unit late Monday afternoon for a last-minute strategy session. I was in the front row, jotting down every word.

"Now, you ends," Tom began, drawing up a formation, "George, Bob, I want you . . ."

I stopped writing on "Bob." Bob (Lilly) wasn't a goddamn end. Bob was a goddamn tackle. Pat was a goddamn end. Tom had privately decided to shift Lilly from his right-tackle spot out to the left-end position and move Ron East in for Lilly. St. Louis was ahead 31–0 before I got into the game.

On Wednesday of the following week Ernie finally commented on the situation: "You play until Cole comes back." Ernie was dejected. We were 5–4, two games behind in the Eastern Division race and fresh from a 38–0 drubbing on national television.

I substituted for Cole in our next three games and proved to be an adequate left defensive end. We won all three games and were off on the first leg of a trip to the Super Bowl. I didn't star in my brief debut, but more important, I discerned a delicate shift in my relationship with my teammates; a measure of respect emerged there . . . something I returned many times over.

It's a nice, comfortable feeling to be respected by your peers; it provides an element of personal security. Playing, and earning that respect, ends the daily struggle to establish yourself psychologically. It is unfortunate that the shared, mutual respect only envelops the starting, contributing players. Lack of ability, an injury, a term on the bench, or some other spiritual or physical absence from the team's daily affairs results in a falling from communal grace. This more or less explains the dissolution of a friendly triad.

The bonds of friendship between Cliff, Charlie, and myself had been forged in response to the ordeal of being one rookie in the horde of rookies that gorge NFL training camps annually. A rookie's life in the context of the organization is at best day-to-day. When one of us had a rough afternoon on the old gridiron, the other two buoyed him up. Similarly, if the day went well, the group supplied the encouragement that did not come from the coaching staff; it was easier to cope with training camp that way. With the season came an element of self-preservation.

Cliff was in Fort Polk several weeks before the Cowboys

finally persuaded the military community down there to free Private Harris for weekend duty on the gridiron. He returned for the New York Giant game and, for lack of preparation and conditioning, was relegated to the specialty units. Cliff observed most of the game from the bench, and he was not pleased with what he saw. He saw Charlie. In Cliff's eyes Charlie had usurped the free-safety position, he had usurped Cliff's social position, and he was wallowing in recognition earmarked for Cliff. Cliff seethed with jealousy and lusted for his lost position.

These developments riddled the relationship. Cliff and Charlie, victims of pride and the glory bug, became embittered rivals. I was caught in the middle. When the season ended, I moved to Nashville.

After years of viewing professional football on television, I had come to the conclusion that playing professionally would be a cool, unemotional experience. My first season was anything but that. To recapitulate:

We made an inauspicious start, racking up five consecutive losses through the preseason. The team was decidedly unsettled. The quarterback, Craig Morton, was getting over shoulder surgery and could not throw without pain; the backup, Roger Staubach, had not yet assimilated the concept of "keying" (observing the opponents' defensive backfield to determine their pass coverage) and was therefore not ready to play. The absence of a clear-cut leader was compounded by a major shift in the offensive line (Rayfield Wright to right tackle, Ralph Neely to right guard) which further disrupted the offensive unit. When films of the preseason were graded, Coach Landry determined that Morton, Neely, and wide receiver Bob Hayes had not played up to their predetermined "performance levels." They were benched. In their respective positions appeared Staubach (ready or not), Blaine Nye, and Dennis Homan.

Staubach lasted two and a half games at quarterback.

Midway through the St. Louis game Staubach, with two crucial interceptions, was lifted in favor of Morton. The team continued to flounder. After the 38–0 slaughter by St. Louis in the ninth game, the problem was obvious. Former Dallas quarterback Don Meredith, in town for the telecast of the game, observed, ". . . there's no leadership out there."

At 5–4 Coach Landry was faced with a decision: he had to either go with Staubach, or lift some of the pressure off Craig by calling his plays. Tom decided on Morton, citing his experience and ability to execute. We beat Washington the next time out, and then handled Green Bay despite an unnerving incident: a felony charge of indecent exposure was filed against starting receiver Lance Rentzel, and we lost him for the duration.

As the stretch drive unfolded, it looked as though we would have to flip a coin with Detroit for a wild-card berth in the play-offs. However, the Cardinals folded. With five games to play they held a two-game lead in the Eastern Division. Subsequently they lost to New York twice; Los Angeles beat the Giants on the last day of the season, and we miraculously won the East.

Craig was still having arm trouble, but the defense, bolstered by the addition of Herb Adderley, was stout, and the offensive running game, featuring Duane Thomas, was unparalleled. We beat Detroit in the opening round of the play-offs 5–0, and then eliminated San Francisco 17–10 in the National Football Conference title game. Our winning string was snipped at eight by the Baltimore Colts in Super Bowl V, about which more later.

When I joined the Cowboys they were a team with a flaky reputation, and our lurching surge to Super Bowl V only provided a higher scaffold from which to tumble; the Cowboys could not win the big one. The fans wondered why. When Lance Rentzel was convicted of a morals charge and shipped to Los Angeles, they had a ready answer. As the dour taste of the Super Bowl defeat seeped into the off-season, the answers multiplied.

Duane Thomas watched $75,000 disappear into the clutches of his agent, a troubled wife, and a rapacious uncle (Sam). Duane consequently became, as Wells Twombly of the San Francisco *Examiner* said, "pissed off at football, and everything else." In Knoxville, Tennessee, Steve Kiner was arrested at a rock concert for "disorderly conduct and resisting arrest." There was an argument over a seat and Steve ended up throwing it at the arresting officer. Meanwhile, Craig Morton was arrested in Dallas and charged with "indecent conduct and abrasive language." The policeman on the scene claimed Craig urinated in the street and began cursing when he was arrested. "Bullshit," Craig said, dismissing the whole affair. It was also disclosed that Craig had required the services of a hypnotist to deal with the pressures of the past season.

I interpreted this string of fiascos as a type of cognitive dissonance . . . a collective restlessness; the emotion generated in Super Bowl V was too great to dissipate in an offseason. Generally when a team loses a football game, the post-game locker room is abandoned like a sinking ship. After this game the veterans stayed for hours mulling the outcome.

It had been a tremendous defensive game. Our offense, directed by Morton, painstakingly built a 6–0 lead on the strength of two field goals. Their efforts were negated by one incredible play: Unitas faded and fired; the ball flew off his receiver's outstretched hand, off Mel Renfro's fingertips, and into the arms of Colt tight end John Mackey. He ran seventy-five yards for a touchdown. The extra point was blocked.

No matter. With the score 13–6, Dallas, the Colts fumbled the second-half kickoff and we drove to their one-yard line. Duane Thomas knifed in for an apparent touchdown, but Mike Curtis of Baltimore knocked the ball loose. Baltimore tackle Billy Ray Smith signaled Colts' ball, and the referee concurred; in fact, Dave Manders, our center, had recovered.

No matter. With the score tied 13–13 we were driving

for the winning field goal. Morton faded and threw high to Danny Reeves, who tipped the ball to Mike Curtis at the Dallas thirty-five-yard line. Baltimore quickly drove into field-goal range, and Jim O'Brien kicked the winner with five seconds left to play.

Chuck Howley, the MVP and only All-Pro participating, felt we had been robbed. "Freak plays . . . freak plays," Chuck said. "Hell, we didn't lose. . . . We won. . . . They just got the title."

Coach Landry echoed Chuck's remarks. "We're disappointed, but not ashamed," he said. "You just can't play better defense than we were playing. . . . My gosh, three tipped passes gave them all their points. . . ."

Lee Roy Jordan was ready to play again . . . right then. "I'm not taking any shit about this game. We'll be back. We've got good personnel, we're playing the defense, . . . all we need is a little better passing game. We will be back."

———————

The off-season workouts commenced in April, and the restlessness turned to grim determination. When training camp rolled around, almost everyone was ready to go. Duane Thomas held out.

Six days into camp Duane held a press conference at the Press Club back in Dallas. His purpose was to explain the reasons for his holdout and hopefully generate some public support. He failed. In the course of his monologue he referred to Tex Schramm, President and General Manager of the Cowboys, as "sick, demented and completely dishonest . . . an ex-sportswriter." Gil Brandt came off lightly as "a liar," and Coach Landry, "a plastic man . . . no person at all." As far as the players were concerned, Duane's attack on the front office elicited a blanch or two, and an occasional "goddamn." When Duane went on to say that the Cowboys would not return to the Super Bowl without his services, he lost a lot of his teammates. "Fuck him" was the overriding response.

The Cowboys were obviously backed into a corner. They shipped Duane, Halvor Hagen, and rookie Honor Jackson to New England for running back Carl Garrett and a number-one draft pick. Garrett was in Thousand Oaks the next day and over a slam-bang game of dominoes, shared his elation at being with Dallas: "An offensive line," he said, "a real, live offensive line."

Thomas lasted not quite twenty-four hours in New England. Upon arrival he refused to take a complete physical, and in his first practice session exchanged pleasantries with Head Coach John Mazur.

"We use a three-point stance here," Coach Mazur coached.

"In Dallas," Duane said, "we keep our hands on our knees so we can watch the movement of the linebackers."

"Yeah . . . up here it's three-point."

"I'm going to do it my way."

Duane was sent to the locker room. He hit the showers, and then the airport. The trade was reworked. Garrett and the number-one draft choice were returned; New England retained Jackson and Hagen, and relinquished second- and third-round draft choices.

Along about this time, Chuck Howley came out of voluntary retirement and joined the squad. The day Chuck returned, Steve Kiner shot in to see Coach Landry and demanded a trade. During the off-season Tom had promised Steve a chance at Howley's position, in view of Chuck's retirement. With Howley back, Steve was faced with another year on the bench; Tom traded him to New England. It was felt that there was some connection between Kiner's trade and the Thomas affair. Duane and Steve were close friends, and Kiner had publicly concurred with Duane's assessment of the front office. Steve Perkins, then of the Dallas *Times Herald*, caught Kiner at the door and questioned him about the situation.

"I can't see it," Kiner answered. "Man, I don't want to

hang around here covering kicks for four years like D. D. Lewis; I want to play and that's all there is to it."

I wanted to play, too—but the "play me or trade me" tactics utilized by Kiner were low on my list of priorities. I wanted to play for Dallas. I came to training camp physically prepared, bound and determined to move in for George Andrie as the Cowboys' right defensive end. I played well in the early weeks of camp—so well, in fact, that Coach Landry spoke to me, man to man, for the first time. I crawled in from practice one afternoon, and in the usual manner, discarded my shoulder pads and squatted in front of an Olympic free-bar. I was going to do a clean-and-press. Tom had just finished gimp-legging a couple of laps; he walked over to me, took off his cap, and wiped his brow.

"Pat, you're moving good out there," he said, and headed for the showers.

My strong determination to be a starting player could be explained somewhat by an innate discomfort in my secondary role as a . . . bomb squadder. Any guilt pangs I felt as a result of my un-American desire to get off the specialty teams * was erased on the opening kickoff of the first exhibition game against Los Angeles. We ambled out for the first kickoff of the new season and I found myself lined up next to Cliff.

"PSSSST . . . CLIFF!" I whisper-yelled. "I'll hit the wedge. You make the tackle."

"Great," he snickered.

The next thing I knew, I was sitting on a bus, sipping a Coca-Cola. Cliff was lodged next to me.

"I'm going to have a good camp this year," I said as a point of conversation.

---

* The specialty teams consist of the punt-return, punt-coverage, kickoff-return and kickoff-coverage teams. A nonstarting player may participate on any or all of these teams.

"Pat . . . we're on our way back to Dallas. Camp is over."

"How did I do?"

The bus moved off in the direction of the airport. Cliff didn't answer. After a time he asked if I remembered the kickoff. I did, but vaguely.

"Well, you hit the wedge real good. . . . Your head slammed right into this guy's knee. You were stretched out, legs crossed, arms folded, for a solid ten minutes; you looked like a product of Marvin's One-Stop Funeral Service. They finally carried you off and put you up under the bench. Tom even came over to talk to you. . . ."

"Again?"

"Yeah. He asked how you felt."

"How did I feel?"

"You said you'd feel all right if the fucking trainers would leave you alone."

"I said 'fucking trainers' . . . to Tom?"

"Yeah. It was great."

The following Monday I visited a head doctor and underwent a battery of tests. The results were conclusive: I would have to beat out Andrie if I wanted off the kickoff teams.

Last year's disastrous defeat at the hands of Baltimore in Super Bowl V posed a formidable task for Coach Landry; he somehow had to rebuild the emotional base of the club and transform it once again into a smoothly operating, competitive unit, capable of steamrolling to Super Bowl VI. Tom chose a spiritual approach. His opening spiel at camp was a reverent discussion, heavily spiked with biblical references, of the past season and all of its frustrations and elations.

"Achievement builds character," Tom explained. "People striving, being knocked down and coming back, . . . this is what builds character in a man. The Bible discusses this at length in Paul. Paul says that adversity brings on endurance, endurance brings on character, and character brings on hope."

The first week of camp Tom sprang a "guest lecturer" program on us. The first speaker in the short-lived series was a man named Hack. Hack specialized in revelations and dope fiends and hailed from San Jose.

"I used to spend a lot of time at home with my family," Hack began "until I became involved with Sergeant Tobias of the L.A.P.D. Tobias is in the juvenile division, and he runs into a lot of troubled kids. 'Hack,' he always says, 'we got problems down here! You better pack your bags and grab a plane. . . .' And I always respond. . . . I just want to help the kids. I find them OD'ed on heroin and ask them if they've accepted the Lord as their savior— and they want to!

"Right now I'd like to introduce you to one of the kids we have helped. This is Peter. Peter is off the hard stuff now and into the Lord and pop wines."

Peter stepped in front of the group and Hack sat down.

"Like . . . I hated my parents, man . . . so I . . . ripped off some . . . wheat germ, . . . but . . . like . . . it didn't work, man . . . so I tried . . . . . and then Hack and Sergeant Tobias saved me, mannnnnnn . . . . . . and that's where I'm at today."

The "guest lecturer" program was subsequently halted and supplanted by the "guest vocalist" program. This program came to us through the combined efforts of Tom and one Billy Zeoli. "Z" (as he affectionately refers to himself) operates out of Chicago and is a purveyor of inspirational flicks. Zeoli made initial inroads with the Cowboy management in 1970 when he approached them with the idea of doing a film on Tom; it would be entitled "A Man and His Men." Coach Landry liked the idea, the film was done, and Zeoli has become a permanent fixture around here.

Billy invariably shows up grinning and shaking hands, reeking of success, affluence, and good news. He seems to draw some kind of psychic energy from the team, and it must be meaningful for him; he has suffered more personal expense and general inconvenience to be associated with this team than any other peripheral person I have yet encountered.

What Billy brought to us was a blossoming star from the underground, pop-gospel segment of the musical jungle. Tom announced that the concert would serve as a change of pace from our grueling training-camp schedule, and at 7:30 P.M. one Wednesday, we all filed into the meeting room. A classy PA system dominated the room: a bevy of microphones was positioned in the center, flanked by two large, efficient-looking speakers; some sophisticated recording equipment was tucked in behind a portable blackboard. Zeoli introduced Dave Boyer, and the show was on.

Dave kicked off the evening of entertainment by relating the long and difficult story of his troubled life. As a youngster Dave wanted to be a pop-singing superstar. He worked hard and got the big break in the form of a gig at the incredible Club 500 in Atlantic City, New Jersey (Atlantic City was big-time in those days). He started drinking, taking bennies, dropping reds, and beating his wife. She left him. The standard show-biz spiral ended when he saw the light, found Jesus, and made up with his wife. He was now in the process of living happily hereafter. "I'm singing for God now," he said.

"At this time," Dave continued, "I'd like to sing several cuts from our first album recently recorded in London for the Reverence label. . . ."

Polite applause.

Dave sang live, accompanied by the recorded backup, for fifty uncomfortable football players stuffed into minuscule desks, sweltering in a college-dormitory lounge. His repertoire consisted of the classic "I Believe in a Hill Called Mount Calgary," the provocative "Happiness Is the Lord," the inevitable "Do You Know My Jesus?" and, for the finale, the scintillating song of our country "America the Beautiful." A wash of embarrassment coated the room. The meeting was adjourned.

Zeoli visited us all in our rooms later in the evening, seeking the consensus on the performance.

"Well, Pat, what did you think of our boy?"

"Great," I lied.

Jerry DePoyster had not applauded after the final selection, and he reported that he was cornered after the meeting by one of the business managers: "Why in the hell didn't you clap after 'America,' DePoyster? What in the hell is wrong with you anyway?"

"I just got back from Viet Nam," was the retort.

Training-camp Saturdays had been good when I was a rookie . . . days to be savored. The afternoon scrimmages always passed quickly; Cliff, Charlie, and I would gorge ourselves at the training-table buffet and wander into town to relax . . . a respite from the tedious affairs of the week.

As the summer slipped by, we had had no choice but to become Conejo Valley connoisseurs. As a result of vigorous, twice-daily observations (i.e., practices), we were eventually able to lecture intelligently on the Conejo Valley meteorological confluence (ironically, there is none—it doesn't even rain). We made definitive studies of Conejo Valley night life; in fact, our greatest strides came in the assorted, sordid, evening interactions with some of the Conejo Valley residents. The brasher members of our rookie contingent discovered early on that the words "Dallas Cowboy" were magic: "Hello darlin', I play for the Dallas Cowboys . . . wanna fuck?" proved to be an effective come-on with many of the local barflies and snuff queens.

The average Saturday-afternoon residents came to recognize us on sight as "some of the Dallas Cowboys," subtitled "Oh . . . Rookies." We in turn spent entire evenings sitting in front of the dormitory recognizing groups of citizens as Conejo Valley residents: "Hey, you guys must be from the Conejo Valley. . . ."

"How in the hell did you know?"

This year's Saturdays have been flavored differently. The second weekend of camp Cliff and Charlie ate hurriedly and roared off to compete for whatever attentions were available in downtown Thousand Oaks. They compete twenty-four hours a day, and I can't handle it. Not again. Being a Dallas Cowboy has lost some of its sheen.

As a rookie I was impressed with my new status. "Dallas Cowboy" meant Super Bowls, choice seats in restaurants, deals on new automobiles—recognition. I was enamored with the situation . . . for a time. I finally noticed that people dealt with me solely on one level—football. It made me uncomfortable. Cliff and Charlie still seem to revel in the aura surrounding those two words, "Dallas Cowboy." Cliff, in particular, seems to derive an inordinate amount of personal fuel merely from the fact that he is, above all, a Dallas Cowboy. We have argued many times the relative advantages and disadvantages of being traded, but for Cliff, the whole concept is tinged with disgrace. "If I'm traded," he said, "it will mean I didn't measure up." I have yet to encounter anyone who plays football with the intensity Cliff does, but he is apparently motivated by fear and insecurity; he is afraid he will somehow lose what he has achieved, his position . . . his badge—Dallas Cowboy.

From a management standpoint, I suppose this is a desirable situation. The Cowboy corporate image has been carefully, lavishly cultivated over a period of years through inordinately close ties with all forms of the media, and with the universities and coaching staffs who supply their talent; today a rookie comes to training camp with the osmotic feeling that the Dallas Cowboys are "it." If the rookie becomes a veteran, he often retains that concept for years. Lee Roy Jordan and Bob Lilly, to name two, played nine or ten years before they discovered they had been blatantly buggered by the front office in all phases of compensation. For an individual who bases the core of his existence on the corporate reflection, the inevitable awakening is a nontrivial jolt.

So Cliff and Charlie were gone for the evening. I opted for the dormitory.

Around 7:30 I came out of my room and surveyed the linoleum corridors. Except for a muffled television broadcast floating down the hall, there was no noise. No one was around. The television set was down in Blaine Nye's room. I strolled down, cracked the door, and peeked in. Larry Cole was asleep in his underwear on the far bed, snoring pleasantly. The TV had turned itself on; the vertical hold, the horizontal hold, and the contrast were all broken; the set was picking up three stations simultaneously. Blaine was lying on his back on the near bed, examining the ceiling.

"Welcome to the Zero Club," he said.

The room smelled like salvation.

I flopped on the middle bed and joined Blaine in his scrutiny of the ceiling. Blaine is a big, blond, overeducated offensive guard from Stanford; if people were cars, he would be a four-wheel-drive International Travelall with interlocking hubs.

"Fuck," he said characteristically. "This is the Zero Club," Blaine made a sweeping gesture with his hand, "and we're organized. I am *el Presidente,* Cole is Vice President, and you are hereby appointed Social Secretary."

"Good," I said, "let's go to a movie."

"Ah. Ah. Ah. Hasty, hasty. . . . Let's think about it; the shock of going to town may be too much for Cole. Round up the transportation and wake us up when you're ready."

Cole snorted. I picked up the telephone and dialed Bob Griffin's room; the scouts rent cars for training camp.

"Grif?" I said confidently, "Toomay here. How about lending me your car for awhile? A couple of us would like to go to the show."

"Who's going?" he asked.

"Oh . . . Nye, Larry Cole, myself."

"Naw," he said, "you shouldn't be caught dead in public with those guys."

Grif had to use his car, so I wandered outside and found Sam Scarber, a rookie running back, climbing into his girl friend's car, headed for town. I asked Sam if he would drop us by the theater on his way and he said he would. I hollered for Blaine, and the three of us wedged into the back seat of the Toyota Corolla. The girl friend drove.

It was an eventful evening. The movie was *How to Frame a Figg*, starring Don Kotts. Cole farted in the middle of it. We walked home.

"You know," Larry said as we trudged through the brush, "Lee Roy, Charlie, Walt, . . . all those studs are out on the town tonight and they probably think they're having a good time: nice restaurants, good wine, live entertainment, but they're not. We are. We're having the good time, aren't we, Blaine? Aren't we having a GODDAMN GREAT TIME!!?"

At that point Larry jumped on Blaine and they fell into the dust in a thundering mass.

The philosophical undercurrents of the Zero Club eddy about the idea of enlightened indifference. The group is dedicated to ennui. Meetings are held sporadically in Blaine and Larry's room, primarily for the comforting air of languor that exists there; the room smells like an overheated TV, and Cole has covered the only window with aluminum foil, effectively blocking out unnecessary, lifegiving sunlight. Thoughts rot as quickly as they are verbalized.

Most organizations contain a built-in pension program for the security of their members; the Zero Club subscribes to Joseph Heller's Boredom Cultivation Plan. It is universally recognized that when someone is enjoying himself, time passes quickly. Similarly, when someone is not enjoying himself, time drags intolerably; it's one of those unfortunate quirks of nature. However, by actually cultivating boredom, one can slow time down considerably, and Zero Club members are able to add years to their otherwise truncated life expectancies.

"Of course, the converse is true for Cole," Blaine said

one day in a half-hearted discussion of the subject. "Time is flying for Larry. . . . Look at him. . . . He's prone . . . . . . and unconscious."

Because of his ability to remain unflappable in the face of fire, famine, pestilence, and the changing seasons, Cole has emerged as the high priest of the Zero cult. Larry's interesting physical appearance (bleached-white hair with matching skin that fades to a light purple in slumber) makes him a perfect nonspokesman for the group. He is for the Zero Club what Buddha was for the Chinese—a model worthy of emulation.

Cole, by his own volition, placed his esteemed position in jeopardy this past off-season. I met Larry at Love Field in July for the flight to camp . . . and he had done the unthinkable.

"Pat," he explained, "I came into a little extra money, and at my wife's behest, I walked into King Size Clothing and said, 'Dress me.' "

They did. Larry was dazzling in a pumpkin-orange sport coat with wide, green, windowpane checks; he sported a brown shirt with green, white, and orange stripes; a pair of lime-green double-knit slacks, black shoes—and a blue tie. Larry's gross tastelessness saved him from imminent disbarment. To reinforce his new image, Cole had also run for a city-council slot in the borough of Bedford, Texas. I pressed him for the election results.

"I got exactly what I wanted," he said. "Defeat."

The exhibition season passed quickly, and as the season opened, we were prepared for good things. Duane Thomas reported he was ready to play, and after being cleared by Pete Rozelle, the Southwest Medical School, and Coach Landry, he was back on the field. "If he can help us win the Super Bowl," Tom said, "he'll be more than welcome." That was the consensus of opinion.

Duane's individual approach to the game had changed. On advice of his counselor, Jim Brown, Duane decided he would only fulfill his contract . . . nothing more. This meant a policy of noncooperation with the press and various club extracurriculars. Duane receded into silence. This caused consternation with the coaching staff, but Duane was communicating in hundred-yard performances, and it was hard to argue with those.

Charlie and Cliff ran the preseason race for the free-safety slot and ended in a dead heat. Charlie retained the position on the basis of experience. I endured the same kind of competition with George Andrie, and we ended up splitting time. This was not entirely satisfactory to either of us, but it was better than not playing at all.

The season rapidly fell apart. After the seventh game we were right where we had been the previous year: a lack-luster 4–3 record, two games behind the division-leading Washington Redskins (6–1), and fresh from a devastating performance in Chicago.

Nothing had gone right in that Bear game. The revolutionary "quarterback shuffle" (Staubach and Morton alternating on offensive plays) did not generate any points; Mike Clark missed three of four field goals (two from inside the thirty); and Cliff fumbled a midfield punt with 1:40 left on the clock.

Herb Adderley slumped exhausted in front of his locker after the game. "Shit," he said to no one in particular. "At times like this I wish I'd gone on . . . and become a pimp."

On Monday, Ralph Neely broke his leg in a motorcycle accident. We were primed for the stretch.

Tom hastily juggled the lineup. Charlie Waters, beset with bad times and big plays, had already been moved out in favor of Cliff. In the wake of the Bear game Mike Clark was waived to the taxi squad, Austrian Toni Fritsch was activated to handle the place-kicking, and Roger Staubach was named the number-one quarterback.

St. Louis was our next opponent and the turning point

for the season. It wasn't an easy game. Midway through the third period our visions of Super Bowl momentarily evaporated; the Cardinals were ahead 10–6 and Jim Hart hit Jackie Smith for a twenty-six-yard touchdown. Fortunately, a holding penalty was called on St. Louis and the play was nullified. A reprieve. With fourth down on the nineteen, a tie score, and 1:43 remaining, Toni Fritsch bounced out to try for the deciding points.

Cardinal linebacker Larry Stallings launched a verbal assault at poor Toni: "Hey, you midget-bastard-kraut, you're gonna choke!! BLOW IT, YOU LITTLE SHIT-HEAD!!"

"Save it," Dave Edwards instructed from our side of the line; "he doesn't understand English."

Fritsch thumped it through and we won 16–13.

"You know, Toni could be a catalyst," Tom said after the game. "One guy can get in a hot streak and you never know what effect it will have on your team. It was great to come back for a win."

Fritsch was a hero in his professional debut; he received three hearty cheers, a game ball, and an avalanche of attention. The coaching staff, sensing a rising star, descended on Toni en masse: they analyzed, categorized, and finalized every aspect of his kicking style; they measured every conceivable angle, azimuth, and abscissa. . . . "Aha!" they said as we approached a crucial showdown with Washington, "Toni has never kicked in the mud!"

They made a mudhole.

Toni stepped into the slime, slipped, and pulled a hamstring. Our catalyst was converted into a training-room fixture.

The rest of this chapter is as follows: we won ten games in a row, including a biological dismemberment of the Miami Dolphins in Super Bowl VI, and became World

Champions. The stretch drive leading to the Super Bowl was a pressure-packed, humorless period, best described in the colorless language of statistics. It is sufficient to say that we were a machine, and we rolled. A collective good-feeling developed then, but it didn't last.

My strongest impressions are from the periphery of the Super Bowl experience. They are scattered and illogical:

(1) I was eerily struck by Tex Schramm's comments in our euphoric post-game locker room: "We'll be back," he said to everyone; "this was only a start. They can't say we don't win the big one anymore. I don't know which big one is left. We're going to be like the Yankees and the Celtics—a dynasty."

(2) The cover of the 1972–73 edition of the Dallas Cowboy press book sported a picture of the Vince Lombardi Trophy flanked by (in descending order of appearance) club owner Clint Murchison, Tex Schramm, and Tom Landry.

(3) I ran into Bob Lilly the morning following the game and he was beaming in the New Orleans sunshine. He asked me how it felt to be a champion, and I had to admit it felt pretty good. Bob went in for breakfast, and I headed for my room. Unaccountably, a line from the movie *Downhill Racer* came to mind. The hero is home in bed convalescing after a near-fatal skiing accident. His father asks him what drives him to compete on that level.

"I want to be a champion," the son answers.

"Son," the father says, "the world's full of 'em!"

3

DYNASTIC DISSONANCE

Have you ever seen a bug in amber?" I asked Blaine Nye as we bussed out of LAX bound once again for Thousand Oaks and another Dallas Cowboy training camp. It was a pertinent question. I was beginning to feel precisely like an encased anthropod—helplessly suspended, not in amber, but in a frozen chunk of time, a Tralfamadorian moment: I have always been on this bus, and, it seems, I will always be on this bus. The exhaust fumes of the Great Western charter have already infiltrated the air-conditioning system and are starting to mingle woth the sour smell of deodorants. The air has effectively turned to syrup. The perspiration trickling down my rib cage is bred from anxiety. California is July-brown.

"Have you ever seen a bug in amber?" I asked Blaine again.

Blaine was asleep. He was always asleep.

The conversation on the bus gave me the distinct impression that no one wanted to be out here, that it was unfair for the season to be rumbling around again so soon. It was yesterday (wasn't it?) that the Dallas Cowboys overcame ten years of exponential frustration through the ultimate experience in professional football, a World Championship. Let us rest our laurels.

Upon arrival in Thousand Oaks we were rushed through a new, elaborate physical and funneled into the first meeting of the new year. Coach Landry excused the rookies and addressed the veterans. He spoke of the magnitude of last season's accomplishment and the tremendous task before us. "No team," he said, "has participated in three consecutive Super Bowls; this is a great challenge for us." He dashed all secret hopes when he stated unequivocally that we could not, under any circumstances, rest on our laurels.

Afterward I plodded over to the campus snack bar and purchased the first root-beer float of the quickening season.

One of the privileges of winning a Super Bowl is the opportunity to kick off the season by playing a charity game with the College All-Stars in Chicago. We have two weeks to prepare, and so far the two-a-day workouts have consisted of standard fare, except for a stretching program headed up by a new defensive backfield coach, Gene Stallings. Everyone is very sore.

Coach Landry is spending most of his time with the defensive unit, as he looks upon the All-Star game as a personal challenge from the collegiate ranks. He feels we must shut down the assortment of option plays * popular in the NCAA, or eventually be faced with defensing them in the NFL.

League rules dictate that the professional team taking part in the game may not have any preparatory scrimmages with other teams before the contest. This leaves us to ourselves. The defensive line is spending its time learning how to evade an offensive tackle's hook block and polish

---

* The quarterback takes the snap from center and moves laterally down the line of scrimmage. He either (1) hands the ball to the fullback, (2) pitches the ball to the trailing halfback, (3) runs it himself, or (4) throws a forward pass.

the optioning quarterback. Tom's thinking is if you eliminate the quarterback, there can be no option.

I was glancing over the rosters of the '70 and '71 Cowboys and was suprised to note an approximate turnover of 25 percent each year. I wonder if winning the Super Bowl will be a hedge against this exodus. Coach Landry so appreciates experience that I would think he would be hesitant to part with any player who contributed to last year's effort. He did trade Joe Williams and Margene Adkins during the off-season draft, and Tony Liscio retired, but those developments weren't particularly surprising. Joe faced stiff competition as a running back, Margene was not adjusting to the complicated offense, and Tony was ready to get out. Eight to ten more people will be going traveling this summer if there is any truth in statistics.

The first casualty of this training camp appears to be Tom Stincic. His severance, if that's what it is, was by his own hand. The only item he left behind was a terse note on top of his Styrofoam cooler addressed to his suite-mate, Billy Truax. "It's all yours, Bill," was all it said. Truax inherits three small cartons of spoiled yogurt and one tired can of Orange Plus.

Stincic hinted at his departure in conversation a few days ago when I innocently asked him how he was doing.

"I'm leaving," Tom answered. "I'm fed up with this shit."

Stincic was Lee Roy Jordan's understudy at middle linebacker, and Lee Roy had been ailing and unable to practice. Stincic had been doing all the practicing.

"It's not really that," he said lethargically. "It's the fact that when the All-Star game rolls around next week, Lee Roy will be out there regardless, and my ass will be back on the bench. Again."

Stincic was certain he had the ability to play regularly

and was anxious to get into somebody's lineup—so he disappeared.

The All-Star game, coming up this weekend, is the first significant event of the new season. It marks the end of two-a-day practices and the official beginning of the 1972 season. Our preparations for this game have been arduous. I can not possibly tolerate watching another reel of Nebraska game film.

We have been watching Nebraska because their head coach, Bob Devaney, will coach the All-Stars and Jerry Tagge, the Nebraska quarterback, will run the attack. Nebraska was primarily a power I-formation team last year and did not extensively utilize the option plays. However, the rumors flowing from the All-Star camp indicate they will test us with every option play available. If there is one play we can now stop, it's that damned option.

On the way back from town last night, Dave Manders and Craig Morton detoured into McDonald's for a late snack. As they were strolling in, they spied John Niland sheepishly ducking out the side door. He had in his hands a sack full of McDonald's finest.

"A-HA!" Manders screamed.

Niland froze.

"You know you're overweight, John," Dave lectured; "those burgers are going to cost you fifty dollars at the weigh-in tomorrow."

"Hurruummmpph," John said.

Niland had been starving himself to get down to playing weight. This was a significant breaking of his diet.

Craig and Dave went back to their room and were preparing for bed when a disturbing noise emanated from the bathroom. It sounded something like "RRHHHAAALLLPPH." Manders tore open the door. Niland was leaning over the commode with a brush handle

jammed down his throat. He was vomiting the ham-
burgers.

"Oh, good Christ . . . ," Dave said.

"You're disgusting," Craig added.

Niland was matter-of-fact. "I can't use the calories," he
said. John brushed his teeth and went to bed.

The College All-Star game had been a traditionally dull
extravaganza and this edition was no exception. We were
rusty, they were tight, and we won with an attitude that
could only be described as disinterest. They attempted the
option play twice, for negative yardage.

The true import of the game, as discerned by our men-
tors, was not disseminated to the players until Sunday's
film session. The defense was praised for beating back that
collegiate monster, the triple option; the offensive unit
was berated for general nonperformance. Tom declared
that we now rank "between twenty-second and twenty-
sixth in the league in total offense." An exceptional feat
considering we are 1–0 and nobody else has played a
game. The point is, obviously, that we would finish last if
we consistently played this caliber of football for the duration of the season. I feel a scrimmage coming on.

My premonitions were right. Denver is bussing up here
on Wednesday from their training headquarters in Pomona, California, for a little scrum.

Gloster Richardson was dealt away tonight to the Oakland Raiders. He came to Dallas last year from Kansas City
in exchange for Dennis Homan, a former number-one draft
pick. Gloster's play last season had been generally considered inconsistent, but he was having an exceptional training camp this go-round. It is well known that Tom's final
criterion in judging a wide receiver is the receiver's will-

ingness to block. This may have caused the demise of
Gloster Richardson in Dallas.

Last night in the offensive line's meeting Jim Myers
asked his first-year men to give their personal evaluation
of training camp.

"Intellectually," began one prize rookie, glowing at the
thought of a multisyllabic word, "it was much more
tougher than I figured."

Duane Thomas has become for the Cowboys what Rus-
sia was for Winston Churchill: the proverbial enigma,
wrapped in a riddle, doused with Tabasco, and stuffed into
a cheese enchilada.

Last year Duane would not speak to the press, nor
would he answer the roll call in team meetings. This season he has thus far maintained that *status quo;* he hasn't
taken any meals with the team, nor has he spoken to the
press or many of his teammates. At mealtime Duane slips
into the cafeteria early and fills a paper bag from a table
stacked with fresh fruit. He then proceeds back to his
room, munching green peaches along the way. Duane is
looking rather svelte these days.

Yesterday he added another straw to the burgeoning
load when he failed to appear at practice. From what I can
surmise, his problem is basic: Duane is still pissed off at
football. As is often the case, simple problems have complex solutions. Duane played the '71 season at a salary of
about $20,000. He felt he deserved a sizable raise after an
awesome year, and the Cowboys suggested $30,000.
Duane was thinking more in terms of $75,000–$80,000.
Needless to say, they have not approached a settlement in
the increasingly strained negotiations.

Duane unquestionably deserves an increase in salary.
Perhaps not the $80,000 he is asking, but a figure in the
neighborhood of $50,000–$60,000 would not be unreason-

able. If he could somehow muster some public sentiment, thereby exerting a little pressure on the front office, he might get some of that money. The problem here is that his actions within the last year have alienated the football public (and not a few of his teammates).

Regardless of any personality quirks, Duane Thomas is an outstanding talent, a premier running back, and a vital part of our football team. He senses this and has said publicly that we will not go to the Super Bowl again without his services. This may or may not be true, but the outside running game was fundamental to our success last season and Duane *was* the outside running attack. One thing is certain: if Tex Schramm chooses not to pay Duane, someone else will jump at the opportunity, and then it will be all up to Duane.

The Denver scrimmage turned out to be an enlightening experience. I expected the Broncos to bus up here with fire in their eyes, ready to rip up the reigning World Champions. After all, John Ralston is at their helm this year, and he is a certified instructor for the Dale Carnegie Institute. I'm not sure if we can cope with that kind of power. We suited up and shuffled out to the practice fields. I glanced over at the Bronco's warm-up procedure and immediately took heart; the Broncos looked like they had run all the way up from Pomona. The day went from good to better.

The drills were organized into a "circus" format: the running games of each club were tested against the respective defenses on one field; the passing games were honed on another. Naturally we of the defensive unit were involved with their running offense. Nobody on either side was very enthusiastic.

My tackle was a big blond guy wearing a practice jersey numbered 73. The huddle broke for the first play and he trotted up to the line of scrimmage. The quarterback barked out some signals; the linemen assumed their stances.

"Away," he whispered.

"What?"

The ball snapped, and the play went away from us. No, I thought, this couldn't be happening.

On the next play the formation's strength was my way. I was sandwiched between the tackle and the tight end.

"Pinch," said the tackle.

"Pinch?" I asked.

At the snap of the ball, I fell right on my face. The tackle and the end jumped on top of me. It *was* a pinch block! This was too good to be true.

The whole afternoon passed in a similar manner: he would call it; I would play it. But one must be judicious in such a situation. If I had taken full advantage of my advance notice and subsequently made a sparkling play, our relationship would have been unilaterally terminated. As it went, neither of us looked too good, but neither of us looked too bad either. We made it through the day with no injuries, no ruffled egos, and no bellowing coaches. There may still be hope.

Duane wasn't present at the scrimmage. He wasn't even in the city. Last night he was swapped to the San Diego Chargers for a wide receiver, Billy Parks, and a running back, Mike Montgomery.

The first half of our meeting this evening was devoted to the Thomas situation. Coach Landry explained that he had desperately tried to save Duane's career: "I talked with Duane for hours, relating to him what he must do to become a part of society. I took him each step of the way, and I felt he was making progress—until he missed the morning meeting and the afternoon practice. I went to see Duane in his room to find out why he had missed the sessions. Duane said that he wasn't paid to attend meetings, he was paid to play on Sunday. I told Duane that he had to follow certain rules to be a part of this team, and he refused. I had no choice but to trade him."

I haven't been close to the Thomas affair over the past several years. The only experience I had with him happened before we were officially with the club. The Cowboys have a rookie orientation period a few weeks after the annual player draft. The rookies fly in for the weekend, work out for two days, and head home. Duane and I were appointed roommates, in accordance with the alphabetical listing. When I went to check out of the hotel, there were thirty dollars' worth of long distance calls charged to my name. Since all the calls were to west Texas, I suspected Duane and refused to pay the bill. When we came back to Dallas from training camp, Duane and I were to be paired again. I balked. Duane persuaded me it had all been a misunderstanding, and the incident was forgotten. I roomed with a kicker named Tom Rogers.

Tonight, with the official, physical severance of Duane Thomas at hand, I found myself admiring him for his particular style. He is unorthodox in everything he does, from his manner of speech to the way he carries the football. He is a state-of-the-art running back, practically elegant; his incredibly deceptive speed is complemented by a precise sense of timing. It was his deceptive speed that Tom Brookshire alluded to in his interview with Thomas following the 1972 Super Bowl. Brookshire asked Duane if he was, indeed, "as fast as he appeared to be." The response: "Evidently."

I also found myself admiring Duane for his strange accomplishment: he seems to have cracked the arrogance that has encased the Cowboy front office for years. He has forced them to do something they did not want to do—to trade him. The Cowboys have never deliberately dumped a first-rate player unless that player was injured, or going over the hill.

The exhibition slate dictates an engagement with the Houston Oilers this weekend on our home (plastic) turf. The heat can be oppressive this time of year in Dallas, so

I'm searching for alternatives to making this trip. I'm not having much luck.

Texas is noted for its grandiose self-image, and true to form, Texans have built the largest sauna bath in the world right in Irving, Texas. It has cleverly been named Texas Stadium. The stadium rises out of the Irving bottomlands looking like a colossal Big Mac: the Irving Cheeseburger, as it is becoming known, home of the Irving Cowboys. Texas Stadium is one of those rare facilities in the nation where spectators, sitting stock-still on their hands, can expect to lose as much weight during the course of a game as the participants.

Last year at this time I was getting my first real shot at a starting position. The golden opportunity was almost the conclusion of an obscure career.

It all started with Lee Roy Jordan. He was injured the week before last year's match with Houston and unable to play. Tom Stincic got the starting nod, and out of deference to his starting position, Coach Tubbs spared him the rigors of playing on the specialty units.

George Andrie was injured also and unable to play. This thrust me into a starting role. I waited all week for Ernie to approach me and let me know I didn't have to worry about the specialty teams. He never did. By game time I was frantic to get off those damn suicide squads. I wanted to be able to concentrate 100 percent on the game, make a good showing, and exert some subtle pressure on George.

I ran under one punt before recruiting John Fitzgerald to fill in for me. Rookie hopeful Ron Kadziel gladly took over the kickoff return and kickoff coverage—he was dying to get on the field. So was Don Talbert, a nine-year veteran who had just joined the Cowboys by way of New Orleans. Don went in on the punt return. He turned out to be my downfall.

When the coaches were grading films they came upon a play in which the Houston punter failed to kick at the proper time. Instead, he stood back there for fifteen minutes and ran the ball forty yards.

"Who missed that easy tackle at the line of scrimmage?"

"Talbert."

"Talbert?" said Coach Franklin. "What in the hell is Talbert doing in there? That's supposed to be . . . uh . . . let's see . . . Toomay!"

After that, they easily discovered the true scope of my substitutions. Coach Landry didn't mention them until the end of the film session, then he began: "In all my twenty-five years in football . . ."

It hadn't been my day on the field either. The man I was playing against was 6-foot-8 Gene Ferguson. He was not particularly agile; he was definitely not quick, just big. I would unleash a fancy move on him, and he wouldn't react. He neutralized me by throwing his large left arm across my chest and grabbing my outside shoulder. I kicked up dirt all afternoon; in twenty-two chances to get the quarterback, I escaped from Fergy four times. That's hard to do.

"Who is the greatest escape artist in the world?" Walt Garrison is great at riddles.

"Houdini."

"Right. So it stands to reason that the greatest reverse-escape artist would have to be you—Dini-hou."

During the summer, the sports section of the L. A. *Times* records in small print the myriad NFL player transactions. Most players scour the column like an obituary page, searching for their friends' names or their own. There was an interesting item today concerning defensive tackle Dave Costa: "Dave Costa was traded today from the Denver Broncos to the San Diego Chargers for complaining about training camp."

The strange events surrounding Duane's stay in Thousand Oaks this year are beginning to come to the surface.

Duane was preceded to camp by a mysterious man who professed to be a friend of his. He was not under contract with the Cowboys, nor was he listed as a possible prospect; he reported that Duane had said he could try out. The mystery man had no idea of the standard procedures in securing a tryout with a professional team. The only thing he seemed really concerned about was his feet. He wondered out loud to Gil Brandt if it would be possible to wear his army boots out to practice rather than his football shoes. "Cleats hurt my feet," he explained. He was sent home on the next plane only to reappear several weeks later with Duane, serving as his spokesman.

Somehow Duane was persuaded to chuck this guy and join the club. The first item on the agenda when you arrive in camp is the physical.

"Hello Duane, you old son-of-a-bitch," Dr. Knight said jocularly, "how in the hell are you?"

The response was stern and bitter: "Don't you touch me until you learn how to talk to me."

It wasn't too many days before Duane tired of training camp and committed the cardinal sins of skipping a meeting and a practice. Coach Landry was concerned. Dan Reeves and Ray Renfro were innocently strolling down the corridor of the dormitory when Tom instructed them to summon Duane. The pair nodded and walked on toward Duane's room.

"You go," said Ray.

"No, you," said Danny.

They flipped a coin and Renfro lost. Ray tiptoed up to Duane's door and tested it. It was locked.

"Damn it all," Ray muttered.

Tap, tap, tap, . . . no answer.

"Duane?" Ray whispered. "Duuuuaaaaaannnne? Are Are you in there, Duane?"

The door flew open.

"Yeah."

"Coach Landry would like to see you."

"I'm not going."

"Oh . . . uh . . . what shall I tell the man?"

"Tell him I'm not coming."

"Well, . . . okay, podna," Ray said, using his favorite expression.

"HEY! Don't give me that 'podna' shit!"

End of dialogue.

Coach Landry visited Duane a little while later. The door was locked again. Tap, tap, tap, . . .

"Duane? This is Coach Landry; are you in there?"

"Yeah. Can I help you?"

"Well, yes. . . . Why weren't you at practice yesterday?"

"Like . . . I didn't feel like it. . . ."

This was the start of the second dialogue. They talked at each other for more than an hour, and Duane became a San Diego Charger.

Cliff is still plagued by the lack of self-assurance which has stalked him since our rookie training camp. It appears to be a chronic ill; success on the field acts as a temporary palliative, but never a complete cure.

Last night Cliff tossed his book-of-the-week selection (*U.F.O Report*) on the floor, switched off his lamp, and took a shot at going to sleep. He wrestled with his blanket for thirty minutes, breathed deeply three times, and gave up.

"Relax," I said. "You worried about Tom?"

In the evening meeting Coach Landry had unexpectedly called on Cliff to explain his assignment on a 48 man-weak pass defense. Cliff had stammered through four wrong answers. Charlie, of course, knew. . . .

"No, . . . it's not Tom, . . . the son-of-a-bitch . . . ," Cliff mumbled, ". . . if only . . . I had . . . hair . . . like . . . Charlie."

Cliff heaved one more sigh and drifted off to sleep.

Toni Fritsch was involved in a minor misadvanture last night. He was on a mission of mercy—down to Orlando's to pick up a pizza for some of the fellows—and the pizza wasn't ready. He waited. It got to be ten thirty, then quarter to curfew. The pizza finally came and Toni sped back toward the campus.

The local sheriff was lying in ambush and clocked Toni at eighty-five miles per hour. Since Fritsch didn't have his wallet or driver's license with him, the officer became suspicious. When the 5-foot-6 native of Austria told the officer that he was a member of the Dallas Cowboys and had to get back to the dorm for curfew, the sheriff handcuffed Toni and took him down to the station.

"Goddom," said Toni when it was all over, "one cold pizza for you bastads cost me six hundred and forty marks!"

Fritsch is vying for the kicking job with Mike Clark and has an excellent chance of taking it. Toni and Mike are equally accurate inside the thirty-yard line, but Toni has the stronger leg and is thus more effective from farther out. Aside from his obvious kicking talents, Toni adds another dimension to the team—some much-needed perspective. Fritsch came to the club as a world-class soccer player, from the European soccer leagues. He wanted to try his foot at booting the strange-shaped American ball. When he arrived Toni spoke no English, and was totally ignorant of the game of football and all its accompanying traditions. However, he did know his own capabilities and what was best for him in terms of conditioning and routine. When Tom instructed him in the weight-lifting program ("The what?" he said), Toni was miffed: "I kick with my foot," he explained, "not with my arms." A point Tom found difficult to argue.

Fritsch pulled a hamstring one day kicking field goals and was promptly dispatched to the trainers for treatment.

"Well, Toni," began Don Cochren, "what you've got there is a mediallateralpostfemuricmusclespasm. What you should do for that is sixtysecondsinthecoldthirtysecond-

sinthehotcontrastcontrastcontrastwillcauseyourcar-
diovascularcalciumtoevaporate. Okay?"

"No," Toni said. "I will take three days off."

He walked out of the training room and took three days
off.

The funniest, most remarkable thing that happened to
Toni occurred back in Dallas. We were at the Cotton Bowl
closing out a practice with some drills for the specialty
teams. The kickoff-return team was working and Toni had
been booming the ball into the end zone.

"Okay, Toni, kick an onside kick," Danny Reeves instructed.

A blank look fell on Fritsch's face, and I knew right then
that he had never in this world heard of an "onside" kick.
Reeves sensed there was a misunderstanding and took
control.

"To-ni . . . I . . . want . . . you [he pointed at Fritsch]
. . . to . . . keeek . . . on-side . . . keeeek!"

Nothing.

Ernie Stautner, a native West Bavarian who knows how
to say "yes" in Spanish, sensed the difficulty and pushed
Reeves aside.

"To-ni," Ernie helpfully began, "we . . . want . . . you
. . . to . . . keek . . . onside . . . keeek [Ernie swung his
foot as if he were kicking]."

There was no response.

Tom by now was upset at the delay in practice and trotted up the field to investigate. Dan and Ernie briefed him
on the problem, and Tom, understanding the difficulty,
took Toni aside.

"To-ni," Tom explained, summoning his best German
accent, "weeeeee . . . wwwwaaaannnnttt . . . yyyooouu
. . . toooo . . . keeeeeeeeekkkk . . .ooonnnsssssssiidde
. . . keek."

Nothing.

Tody Smith discreetly ducked out of camp today and
headed for the lights of Los Angeles, apparently for a mul-

tiplicity of reasons. During the off-season he destroyed his knee in a pickup basketball game, and it has been slow to come around. Ernie has been pushing him hard in practice, and the trainers have been on his ass also. Tody believes the staff has been notably lacking in compassion. The situation was further compounded by the fact that although Tody was not expected to play in the upcoming Houston game, he *was* expected to make the trip to Dallas. He preferred to stay in California for amorous reasons, and it looks as if he will.

Tom has taken an immediate and firm stand on the Smith situation. Obviously he is concerned about the atmosphere of disintegrating team morale perpetrated by Duane Thomas. Since Tody's value to the club is in terms of his potential, not of proven experience, he may very well find himself in the meat grinder for dissatisfied ballplayers, being processed into mindburgers for the rest of us.

Tom is prepared to sacrifice somebody. He mentioned tonight that Tody, or anybody else who chose to walk out of camp, would be subject to the following consequences: (1) a two-hundred-dollar-per-day fine, and (2) a position on the Cowboys' reserve list, at no pay, for a period of time not to exceed infinity. It's a damn fortunate thing that we had this meeting tonight; I didn't realize all these options were available to us.

The continuing saga of Duane Thomas . . . continues. He has yet to report to the Charger camp. He requested some time to return to Dallas and untangle some personal problems. Duane boarded the plane, selected his seat, sat down, and flipped on his radio–cassette player. Loud. As the jet taxied into take-off position, the stewardess asked him to turn it off. He didn't. In a few minutes she asked him again, and again he refused. The captain came back and asked him; Duane still refused to turn off his machine.

The plane taxied back to the gate, and the sky marshals came aboard and took him away for questioning.

The NFL obituary column reported today that Steve Kiner was traded from the New England Patriots to the Miami Dolphins for one Bill Griffin. On the surface this appears to be a bad move on New England's part. Whereas Kiner was voted their MVP last year, Bill Griffin was cut by Dallas and ended up on Miami's taxi squad. Steve spent his rookie season in Dallas and was considered hero material, but he did not want to sit around and wait for Chuck Howley to retire so he requested a trade. He went to New England for an undisclosed draft choice.

For all his problems and impatience, Steve pulled an unprecedented coup during his season in Dallas. On one bleak Wednesday morning in the midst of a torrential rainfall, Kiner pulled into the field-house parking lot and scanned the area for a parking place. Visibility was near zero, what with the sheets of falling rain and the limited windshield area peculiar to 1964 Volkswagens. He finally spotted a place close to the door, in fact, adjacent to the door. Steve reported to the meeting with nary a drop on him.

Naturally, the usurped parking place belonged to Coach Landry, who was consequently forced to walk a city block in the deluge. He walked into the meeting, wet to the bone, and looked Kiner right in the eye: "I like a guy who lives dangerously," he said—and the place fell out laughing.

"I've noticed a lot of you guys reading those western novels," Tom began the Houston pregame talk. "Football is very comparable to the basic plot of those books; particularly, our position as defending World Champions is comparable to the situation of the gunslinger. Everyone wants a piece of that gunslinger; he's got to be constantly on the alert and always prepared—if he makes a mistake, he's dead. I think you can see the similarity of our positions. If we don't get ready for each and every team on our schedule, we will be stripped of our title. It starts out there tonight with Houston."

"I didn't think he had time to read that shit," Charlie Waters mumbled as we headed out the door.

We won the game 26–24 in a ho-hum affair. Robert Newhouse, a rookie fullback from the University of Houston, ran very well in the contest. He reminds the old-timers of Charlie Tolar, formerly of the American Football League Oilers. When Tolar played, he was known as the "human manhole cover" because of his size. Newhouse is right down there with him; Robert's 203 pounds are packed on a 5-foot-7-inch frame. He easily has the largest thighs, and the widest feet (over five inches) on record. After hitting Newhouse last week in practice, Dave Edwards, speaking through the earhole of his helmet, noted that "tackling Newhouse is like tackling a shot put."

August 6. Los Angeles is our next opponent, so we will be heading back to Thousand Oaks again, cutting our stay in Dallas to two days. It's probably just as well. The temperature here yesterday was a blistering 102 degrees; too damn hot to get any decent work in.

The cafeteria cuisine provided for us would scarcely tempt the palate of an epicurean. In fact, at times it is difficult for even the most devoted glutton to raise hand to mouth. Once a week the master chef prepares a potpourri of the past week's remaining delicacies, and tonight was one of those special evenings.

"Well," said Walt, eyeing the slop, "looks like we're back to the star of *Stagecoach*."

"Ann-Margret?" I was confused.

"No. Slim Pickens. I'll have some from that trough there, . . . please."

George Andrie has been experiencing severe pain in his back and has consequently been unable to participate in practice drills. "Rest and some X rays," prescribed the doctors, and George has been resting nicely.

Yesterday they finally got around to taking those X rays, and the results were not good: the pictures showed that George is suffering from a cracked vertebra and a narrowing disk. George's back has been bothering him since last year. He complained specifically about his problem in the course of this year's induction physical, yet got no satisfaction. After the first practice session he was bedridden, and it was not until today that the true scope of his injury was known.

The Cowboys, in consequence of their excellent draft selections through the years, are not blessed with a great number of journeyman ballplayers. In fact, there is only one man in camp this year with a sufficient number of qualifying references—Don Talbert. Talbert started with the Cowboys in 1961, went to Atlanta in the expansion draft of 1966, to New Orleans in 1968, and back to the Cowboys again in 1971. Don (also known as Mouther) is a solid offensive tackle; however, his true forte is drinking many cases of beer and relating outrageous tales. His unique feel for the four-letter Anglo-Saxon monosyllable (or combinations thereof) and his precise sense of comic timing enable him to come up consistently with the wrong words at the right time. This characteristic is discreetly shown in the classic Don Talbert anecdote.

One off-season Don and Dave Edwards were engaged in selling high-capacity coffee machines to various Dallas business concerns. The lead for this particular day had been a north Dallas bank, and luckily they captured the bank president in the parking lot as he was escaping for the afternoon.

"Good afternoon, sir. I'm Dave Edwards and this is my partner, Don Talbert. We felt you might be interested in purchasing one of our . . ."

"Gee, guys, I'm on my way to an important meeting downtown and I really don't have a lot of time. I'm going to say that, for now, we'll just have to pass on it."

"All we're asking is just a few minutes sir. This coffee machine is one of the finest . . ."

"Fellows, I'm sorry, but we really can't justify such a purchase right now. We're just going to have to pass on it for the time being. Maybe you can come out and see me next month."

"Sir, I don't think you realize the true value of our . . ."

"I'm sorry. We're just going to have to pass on it."

The banker made a move for his car, but Talbert was right there peering into his face.

"Well, pass on . . . motherfucker," Don suggested, opening the poor man's car door. And he did.

Don demonstrated last night that he is the veritable encyclopedia of NFL folklore I expected him to be. Primed with several beers, he easily filled the better part of two hours with off-the-wall anecdotes. The highlights included a glimpse of the real Norm Van Brocklin, a taste of the bombastic New Orleans Saints, circa 1968, and a sample of the tales that have transformed Doug Atkins into the living legend that he is.

The evening began as a casual bitch session revolving around the usual topics—the Cowboys' torturous post-game film sessions, Tom's absolute dominance of the club—but then Talbert's eyes lit up. "Goddamn, you should have been in Atlanta," he said, and off he went.

"The film sessions in Atlanta were down in the guts of

1. Training camp: the doors are locked...

2. ...but the windows are open.

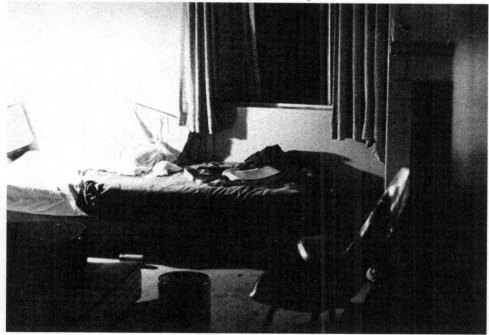

3. Singing for your supper.

4. Ernie Stautner: one of the few remaining intellectuals in professional football.

5. Walt Garrison: a new knife, a mess of basswood, and a headful of snuff.

6. Cliff Harris (left) and Charlie Waters. PHOTO BY RUSS RUSSELL

7. Harris and Waters converge on Rashad of the Cardinals. PHOTO BY JOHN MAZZIOTTA

8. The author. PHOTO BY RUSS RUSSELL

9. The author with Sonny Jurgensen of the Redskins: quarterbacks make strange bedfellows.   *Washington Star* PHOTO BY RANDOLPH ROUTT

10. Larry Cole unwinds after a harrowing day (hair by Waring Blender).

11. Lee Roy Jordan.

12. Dan Reeves (right) with Mike Montgomery. PHOTO BY RUSS RUSSELL

13. Bob Lilly bores in on Cardinal Jim Ray Hart. PHOTO BY RAY ADLER

14. Duane Thomas. PHOTO BY JOHN MAZZIOTTA

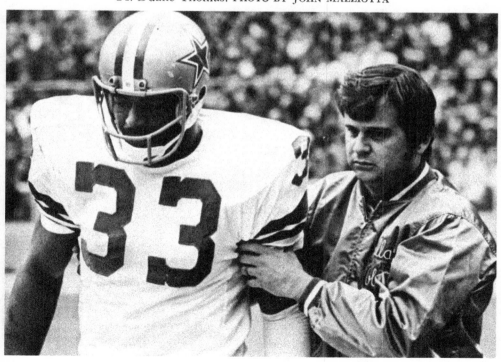

15. Larry Cole and Blaine Nye: two-thirds of the Zero Club.

16. If you can keep your head while those around you are losing theirs...

PHOTO BY RUSS RUSSELL

17. Jethro Pugh. PHOTO BY RUSS RUSSELL

18. George Andrie, age 30.

19. Garrison and Nye have deceptive speed: they are a lot slower than they appear to be. PHOTO BY RUSS RUSSELL

20. Craig Morton and Coach Landry: a failure of communications. PHOTO BY JOHN MAZZIOTTA

21. Gil Brandt and Tex Schramm. PHOTO BY JOHN MAZZIOTTA

22. The Cowboys' computer strikes again.

23. Robert Newhouse misses a tough catch. PHOTO BY JOHN MAZZIOTTA

24. Smasher Asher. PHOTO BY RUSS RUSSELL

25. Mike Clark (foreground) and the man who replaced him, Toni Fritsch. PHOTO BY JOHN MAZZIOTTA

26. Our mentor.

27. Rayfield Wright and Ralph Neely. PHOTO BY JOHN MAZZIOTTA

the stadium," Don explained. "Van Brocklin would come in, fluff his goddamn pillow, lay down on the floor, and roll the film. I remember we had played Pittsburgh's big ass in the mud on the previous Sunday, and they had whipped us pretty good. . . ."

Things began to get pretty tense during the first reel of film. The defense had been on the field for most of the first half because of the incredible impotence of Atlanta's offense, and Van Brocklin was loosening up his vocal cords. One particular offensive series stood out in Don's mind. The first play of that series was a basic trap play: Steve Duich pulled out from his guard position and ran full speed at the mammoth Pittsburgh defensive end. He hit the end and imploded. The guy didn't even flinch, and Duich crumbled to the ground like a sack of wet flour. Loss of two yards. The second play called for Steve to fire out at the big tackle across from him and blow the large fellow out of the hole—the ball carrier would follow. Well, the tackle was so big that when he hunkered down in his stance, he sank ankle-deep in the mire. Duich hit with such impact that he enveloped the guy like a limp tortilla, and slipped harmlessly into the mud. The tackle swallowed the ball carrier and it was third and fourteen. Van Brocklin went berserk.

"TURN ON THE LIGHTS!!" Norm screamed. "TURN ON THE GODDAMN LIGHTS!! Duich, where in the hell are you? DDDUUUIIIIIIIIICCCHHHH!!"

"Here, sir," Duich mumbled meekly.

"You know what, Duich?" Van Brocklin said calmly. "You know what you're like, son? DO YOU?!"

"No sir."

"You're like birdshit, Duich," he explained. "All you do is hit . . . and splatter."

Talbert's next stop was New Orleans. It was not much of an improvement; however, he did fall in with some better-known company in the form of Billy Kilmer and Doug Atkins. Tom Fears was the coach then, and it was his custom to devote a certain amount of practice time each week to the specialty units. In these specialty-team drills Fears would, for example, call out the punt-coverage team, and the appropriate players would line up in their respective positions and cover a punt. All the other players would queue up behind the first team and take their turns at covering. If a player—Kilmer, for instance—who had been on that first unit was unable to cover the kick due to an injury, Fears would say, "Kilmer's down," and the backup player would take Bill's place in the drill.

One fine day the practice schedule called for just such a specialty period.

"All right, men," Fears announced, "we need work on our kickoff coverage. Let's go!"

The players dispersed, and Coach Fears walked down toward the opposite end of the field. Richard Neal, the big defensive end, was nursing a sore knee he had acquired the previous weekend and was unable to participate. Coach Fears noted this from his position and blew his whistle.

"All right!" he yelled. "Neal's down!"

Nobody moved.

"Goddamn it," he shouted, "NEAL'S DOWN!!"

The players began looking around for some hint of what to do. A few of them were beginning to kneel down.

"NO, NO, NO!" he was bellowing by this time. "STAND UP!!" Wild gestures. "STAND UP!!"

The five or six kneeling players stood up.

"Now," he said, gathering composure, "I said *NEAL'S DOWN!!*"

And everybody knelt.

Doug Atkins was a member of that crew, playing his sixteenth or seventeenth season. He was a tremendous man, 6 feet 8 inches tall and close to 300 pounds; yet he was unnaturally agile. He was also inordinately strong and unusually mean.

"He put me on roller skates," Don said. "He would literally lift me up and rifle me at the quarterback."

"When you say he's ornery . . ."

"Atkins was with Chicago before he came to New Orleans," Don said. "Practice was about to get under way at Wrigley Field one day and Doug was nowhere to be seen. Zeke Bratkowski was sent to look for him, but he couldn't find a trace. Bratkowski was reporting back to George Halas when a gunshot rang out, then another. Feathers were drifting down from the stadium roof. Atkins was up there shooting pigeons with a .22 rifle. One of the birds had shit on his car."

Atkins bore no love for his black brethren. At curfew time in the New Orleans training camp, Atkins would appear in the corridors of the dormitory, butt-naked, with a .44 Magnum holstered about his waist. "NO NIGGERS ON THE HALL AFTER ELEVEN," came the announcement, and Atkins was on patrol. As the story goes, only one black man dared venture out of his room and that was Ernie Wheelwright, a 250-pound, bad-ass fullback. He would also be butt-naked with a pistol on his hip, and they often passed each other in the hallways:

"Hello, Doug."

"Oh hey, how ya doin' there, Ernie . . . ?"

Gene Stallings was hired during the off-season to move in for Bobby Franklin and assume the defensive backfield coaching responsibilities. Franklin, in a classic application of the Peter Principle, was laterally arabesqued out to a spot created especially for him: Specialty Team Coach and Person in Charge of Exchanging Scouting Film with Other Clubs. Stallings comes to the Cowboys with a Bear Bryant background and seven torturous years of practical experience at Texas A. & M. He has not been enthusiastically received by his new charges. The main question, still partially unanswered, is how Gene Stallings a former head coach from the deep south with no professional experience, will handle the Cowboys' seasoned secondary—Mel Renfro, Cornell Green, Herb Adderley, and Cliff Harris.

So far he is running them into the ground and boring them with fundamentals.

In preparation for this week's game we have been scrutinizing last year's Los Angeles Ram game films. I'm not sure what to make of Roman Gabriel. On the strength of pure physical dimensions'—6 feet 4 inches, 225 pounds— he ought to be playing in the line with the rest of the big fellas. Gabriel plays quarterback. I think the whole secret of his success lies in his name; if his mother had named him Bruno, or Butch, . . . or Rock, he probably would have made a damn fine tackle. But she held out for Roman, and it is obvious that anyone named Roman can't play in the line.

When you think about it, many players have been plagued with similar name problems, and similar fates. Who can forget the fine passing offense of the Cleveland Browns as generated by quarterback Milton Plum and wide receiver Gail Cogdill? Solely because of their names, those poor bastards were relegated to playing the glory positions through their entire careers.

Since the Rams have been under the direction of Tommy Prothro, they have taken to flip-flopping their offensive line. Most teams leave the linemen in one position and move the tight end around as required for formation strength. The Rams designate one entire side of the line the strong side, and send them to the strength of the formation as called in the huddle. Similarly, the other side of the line is designated the weak side, and they proceed to the weak side of the formation. This significantly complicates the defensive lineman's preparation. He must now study the habits of two offensive linemen instead of the customary one. It would seem that the Ram assignments would be equally complicated. However, at this stage of the exhibition season, they couldn't care less. The Rams are like that.

The two tackles our defensive ends will be concerned with are strong tackle Harry Schuh and weak tackle Charlie Cowan. Cowan is a large subtle player and a master of position and timing. Schuh very closely resembles the Incredible Hulk: he is one huge, pulsating muscle. His idea of pass blocking is a crunching bear hug followed by a knee to the groin and a forearm to the chin. "It's rough down here in the pit," he's fond of saying to rookies, and they always agree.

Judging from what happened to Lonnie Leonard today, the Cowboys are once again excelling in their quest to ease and eventually eliminate the friction inherent in player-management relations. Leonard, a rookie from North Carolina A. & T., sauntered home from practice in the usual way; he trudged slowly up to the dormitory, checked the mail table and message board, and proceeded up to his room to wait for dinner. He received two letters, both from home, and a telephone message that said, "Call collect (716) 856–1567." He did, and the voice down the line answered, "Good evening, Buffalo Bills Football Club . . ." Lonnie was instructed to take the next plane east. Buffalo had picked him up on waivers the previous day.

Jim Murray, the eminent syndicated sports columnist of the Los Angeles *Times*, phoned Blaine this evening to line up an interview for tomorrow afternoon. Blaine agreed, hung up the phone, and withered into a panic. Jim Murray is widely known for his probing wit and sarcastic pen. His request for an interview with Blaine was based on a scathing letter Jim had received from Blaine's mother. "You clowns never cover the local boys!" was what she wrote, and Jim Murray has been waiting to meet this Blaine Nye ever since.

The second part of the problem stems directly from Blaine's overeducation. He has a master's degree in physics from the University of Washington and he is currently pursuing an M.B.A. at Stanford. You would expect a man with those credentials to come up with some fairly pithy statements in the course of an interview, but Blaine has no confidence in his spontaneous wit. When one has no confidence in one's spontaneous wit, one must prepare; we proceeded to the local tavern for a session of preparation. The goal for the evening was to anticipate Mr. Murray's questions, invent some clever retorts, and get drunk in the process.

Larry Cole came up with the concept of "regional appeal" in football.

"The psychological emanations from a given population sample vary according to the geographic location of the sample," began Larry, showing off a tri-university education.

"Huh?"

"Different strokes for different folks," Larry clarified. "People from the south and southwest seem to prefer linebackers, those no-nonsense players who are concerned more with the hit . . . than the game itself. Folks from the northern quarter seem to prefer the big-hog linemen, the big boys who eat too much silage and love to play in the mud. The west coast has always been partial to the Hollywood slots, quarterback and wide receiver. I even heard that high-school coaches had difficulty fielding teams last year—every kid who tried out was six feet two, a hundred and ninety-five pounds, and a quarterback!"

We all agreed on the relative merits of the "regional appeal" doctrine, but we also realized that the possibilities of Murray asking Blaine about anything as remote as "regional appeal" were slim indeed. Larry and I left Blaine to his own devices.

Tom Stincic was traded to New Orleans for a third-round draft pick.

"Cornell, this is just a little thing," Coach Stallings coached, "but whenever you come out of the defensive huddle, you'd best back out of there so you can see if the opposition is trying to slip in a substitute on you."

"Damn, man," Cornell said later, shaking his head. "I've been in this league for twelve years. It took me one year to learn how to put on my equipment and another five to learn how to backpedal. Now, when I'm ready to sit back and enjoy the last couple of good years, I get a rookie coach who ends up trying to tell me how to pop out of my own huddle. Sheeeit!

Coach Stallings, despite an occasional *faux pas*, is becoming increasingly popular with his players. They are discovering that Gene is fair, hardworking, and willing to talk straight from the shoulder. If Coach Stallings does, indeed, turn out to be communicative, he will be a welcome addition to our otherwise tongue-tied and mesmerized staff. For years the chief mode of communication around here has been the rumor.

We beat Los Angeles 27–10, but it was a Pyrrhic victory. On third and two at the three-yard line Roger Staubach faded to pass and was pressured from the pocket. Roger ran to his left and sprinted for the flag in the corner of the end zone. Marlin McKeever, eyeing Staubach and moving laterally from his middle-linebacking position, calculated the collision for the two-yard line. Roger, acutely aware of McKeever and his malicious intent, adroitly avoided the sideline and buried his shoulder into the big fellow. Staubach bounced harmlessly to earth, his right arm limp, his shoulder askew, and "out for the year" etched into his face.

Dr. Knight performed a successful operation (acromioclavicular), and Craig Morton stepped out of the shadows to assume the duties of quarterback.

I do not look forward to playing New Orleans in Tulane Stadium this weekend. The Sugar Bowl is a rotting, rusting edifice that lends itself nicely to the large numbers of screaming, drunken Cajuns who congregate there for Saint games. To get from the locker room to the playing field is a fundamental survival test in itself:

"Gimme your chin strap!!"

"Your helmet!! Your helmet!!"

"Get away from me you little bastards!!"

"I GOT A HANDFUL OF HIS JERSEY!!"

The relative security of the playing field, once reached, is quickly forgotten—other things vie for attention. The heat . . . is oppressive; you notice it first through your shoes, but before you can brood about the heat, the humidity slaps you in the face like a wet towel. After the game, win or lose, you are pelted with ice, spit, and an occasional beer. I always take a quick shower, jump on the first available bus . . . and sit, sweating, in the gnarled traffic.

It wasn't that way in college. My last year in school we took on the Greenies of Tulane in the Sugar Bowl. We played before a reverse capacity crowd, 75,000 empty seats, in the most surrealistic experience of my football career. A couple of days before the game several of Vandy's stalwarts were lolling around Jerry's Pub in Nashville, downing some brew and studying the week's betting line. Vanderbilt was a three-point favorite.

"We can beat them sumbitches by more than three," Neal Smith announced. He circled Vanderbilt and two other favorites on the card and plunked down ten dollars. Homer, the bartender, took the ten-spot and gave Neal a copy of his selections.

"Goddamn, you're right," John Miller said. "Give me one of them sheets, Homer." Miller made the same selections and plunked down his life's savings, twenty-five dollars.

If a fellow picks three out of three games correctly on the pink card, he stands to triple his money. Miller began counting his impending windfall.

Late in the third quarter, things weren't looking too bad. The scores of the other games were in, and everyone was two-for-two. By the fourth quarter, however, a major problem had developed: we were losing our game, and time was growing short. In fact, it was fourth and fifteen on our ten with less than two minutes to play. In a last-ditch effort, Dave Strong went as deep as possible and Denny Painter threw it as far as he could. Two Tulane defenders leaped beautifully to make the interception—and missed. Dave scooped the tipped ball from his shoelaces and scampered the remaining fifty yards to score. The five hundred Cub Scouts in attendance booed. We were comfortably ahead by four.

With thirty seconds left in the game, we got possession of the ball deep in our own territory again. Painter called time-out. "MILLER!" It was Coach Pace. Miller was the backup quarterback and Coach Pace was carefully instructing him. John sulked back to the bench, the boys gathered round.

"You're not going to believe this," John stammered, his voice cracking. "That son-of-a-bitch wants me to go into the game, take the snap from center, run around for as long as I can, and fall in the end zone for a goddamn safety."

John replaced Painter at quarterback, did as he was told, and dropped a veritable fortune; we were favored by three points, we won by only two. Miller was roundly chastised, but the Cub Scouts would have been proud.

The severity of a team crisis is directly proportional to the fluctuations in Coach Landry's otherwise ironclad schedule. On big trading days Tom sometimes gets involved with the necessary manipulating and maneuvering, and will be a few minutes late for practice. Today, in an unprecedented deviation from routine, he missed the entire session. His concern is depth at quarterback.

In a move to shore up that position, Danny Reeves has temporarily relinquished his coaching duties to become a full-time backup quarterback. His position is tenuous, however. From a medical standpoint, Danny is not a good risk; he's got the knees of an old giraffe. In light of this, Coach Landry announced this morning that the Cowboys are in the market for an experienced quarterback, and that Reeves would be serving only in the interim. Unfortunately, interconference trading is over, and Tom is limited to dealing with the twelve other NFC teams. A veteran quarterback will not come cheap.

It is interesting to note the psychological effects a Super Bowl has on a team and its collective sense of well-being. Bill Gregory, John Fitzgerald, Ike Thomas, and Calvin Hill are all expecting new additions to their families. Toni Fritsch and Rayfield Wright have already been blessed. Dave Edwards and Billy Truax are building new homes; Cliff Harris has bought one, and Lee Roy Jordan and John Niland are looking (in the hundred-thousand-dollar bracket). The winner of the Dallas Cowboys "Stimulate the Economy" sweepstakes, however, is none other than Larry Cole, the dynamic resident and financial pillar of bountiful Bedford, Texas. In six short months, Larry, a perennial leader in rural conspicuous consumption, has impregnated his wife, purchased a new, medium-priced, American luxury car, constructed his second custom home in eighteen months, and made ten Tarrant County plumbers moderately wealthy. In recognition of Larry's possession of "economic impact," he has also been selected as the entire Bedford Chamber of Commerce, and awarded by the grateful citizenry five hundred dollars in bonus monthly payments.

Bob Asher spent most of his first two years with the Cowboys in the company of the medical staff, trainers Don Cochren and Larry Gardner, and team physician Marvin Knight. Bob had knee problems. In 1970, in a game with St. Louis, Bob replaced me on the kickoff team. I had gone off after taking a knee to the ribs. Bob went in on the next kickoff and made it all the way to the twenty-yard line without being hit. The ball carrier ran toward him, Bob planted his foot to change direction, and his knee buckled. He was out for two years.

Under Cochren's tutelage, Smasher devoted this year's off-season to getting himself ready for big things. He reported to training camp with the rookies to prove his dedication, and when the call went out for physicals. Bob was at the head of the line. Dr. Knight casually approached Bob, squeezed his giant biceps, and said, "Son, . . . you ever play any football?"

Undaunted, Asher charged into two-a-day practices with a vengeance. The first day he looked great. The old confidence was coming back—fast. He pulled Coach Myers aside and vowed that, come September, he would be the startling left tackle. The following day, Bob seriously wrenched his left knee. He was helped from the practice field into the training room. Dr. Knight rummaged through his bag, produced a long, thick needle, attached a half-gallon syringe, and pumped Asher's knee full of cortisone.

"Now, Bob, do you think you can do a half-assed job in that scrimmage this afternoon?" Dr. Knight asked.

Asher had fainted.

Bob was our guest for dinner last night, and in the course of the evening's conversation he discussed, at length, his dissatisfaction with playing for the Cowboys and living in Dallas, and the possible benefits of a trade.

"Anywhere," he said, "but a team like Chicago. The Chicago Bears are twenty-sixth on my list."

This afternoon I was home for lunch and received a telephone call from Smasher. He was calling from a doctor's office downtown, and he informed me that he had just been traded . . . to the Chicago Bears. In fact, he had just had an interesting long-distance discussion with Abe Gibron, the Bear's head coach:

"Bobby? This is Abe Gibron, head coach of the Chicago Bears. How'd you like to come up here and play some football for me? Before you answer, I want you to know that I will not go through with this deal unless you are a hundred percent in favor of it. Understand?"

"Uh . . . yes . . . this is nothing personal coach . . . but . . . uh . . . there are a lot of places I don't want to be right now . . . and Chicago . . . is all of them."

"That's fine Bob. We'll see you up here on Tuesday."

Asher was surprised and a bit hurt by the affairs of the day. He spent the entire morning in the examination room of an orthopedic surgeon who had been selected by the Bears to examine him thoroughly and report his findings. Ironically, Bob said, the morning physical, courtesy of the Bears, was more thorough than any he had had in all his injured days as a Cowboy.

When the trade went through, Coach Landry, who had been around most of the morning lubricating the process, offered Smasher a ride back to the Cowboy offices so he could pick up any money owed, etc. The situation was awkward. As a point of conversation, Asher asked Tom, an ostensibly pious man, how he rationalized the manipulation of his players and their families as required of an NFL head coach. Tom did not reply. Asher boarded the next plane for his home in northern Virginia.

The Bears, in exchange for aging quarterback Jack Concannon, got Bob Asher, Bill Line (a rookie defensive lineman), and a second-round draft choice.

There are four weeks left in the exhibition season.

Tom announced today that Sid Gillman will reluctantly relinquish his cochairmanship with Ermal Allen of the Research and Development Committee (with responsibility for scouting, grading film, etc.) and assume the on-the-field coaching responsibilities for the offensive backfield. This new development, coupled with the acquisition of Concannon, has placed Danny Reeves in the expendable column.

Just prior to the Concannon trade, Coach Landry requested Dan's presence in conference. In the meeting Tom told Reeves that Sid was to become the offensive backfield coach and that Dan could become the third-team quarterback, if he so desired. His other alternatives . . . were not made clear.

This is an incomprehensible ploy. Reeves is intelligent, articulate, young, with tremendous potential ("remarkably immature," Gil Brandt would say later). He came out of South Carolina in 1965 as a free-agent quarterback with nothing going for him; he didn't have the arm to make a pro quarterback, he was too small to play running back and too slow to play split receiver. Reeves made up for his lack of ability with savvy, stuck as a running back, and eventually reached fifth on the list of all-time Dallas rushers. Through the years Reeves has personified the Dallas Cowboys: handsome, charming; a free agent who made good; a man growing with the club and the community. The Cowboys have cultivated him since his rookie season; yet, in a calculated move, they have replaced him with a sixty-two-year-old transplant, Sid Gillman. This is carrying Tom's premium on experience doctrine a bit far.

The only observation I can make is a subtle and complex one; generally when a team participates in a World Championship game, a significant number of that team's assistant coaches are hired away during the ensuing off-season. The Cowboys have participated in two consecutive Super Bowls, yet not a single member of our coaching staff has departed for greener pastures. Instead, we lose our scouting personnel, the people who know talent. This indicates that our staff is not of the highest caliber, and when you examine Tom's hiring policy, it is evident that this situation came about by design. He requires unthinking, organization types who will not assume responsibility, but will implement his instructions to the letter. This role requires an individual who has been beaten down in his previous work and is thus sufficiently primed for a passive position. Jim Myers was canned by Texas A. &. M. before he became the Cowboy offensive line coach in 1962. Gene Stallings had been fired by the same school when he moved in this year as defensive backfield coach. When Ernie Stautner hired on as defensive line mentor in 1966, he had been freshly dumped by the Washington Redskins, one of the worst teams in football at that time. The reshuffling of Bobby Franklin's duties to make room for Stallings in effect labeled Franklin too as incompetent. The last thing Tom seems to want on his staff is a young, bright coach with ideas. Reeves is benefiting accordingly.

Game day. A team meeting was called this morning to clarify once and for all the raging white-shoe controversy. Billy Parks has been agitating for the right to don white shoes on game days. Until today, however, Tom held firm to the black-shoe tradition established with the club's inception.

"There are still some teams around the league who wear strictly black shoes," Tom began, "the Los Angeles Rams for instance, the Baltimore Colts, . . . THE WASHINGTON REDSKINS; but we checked on seventeen teams and discovered that ten of them wore some mixture of shoes." (Research and Development at work here.) "Last year I came across too tough on the shoe issue," Tom continued. "This year I've changed my thinking. When white shoes first came out, they were worn by individuals, not team people. I think things ahave changed now, so it's going to be up to you."

The coaches left and Lilly took the floor.

"All for black shoes?"

Truax . . . Garrison . . .

"All for white shoes?"

Nobody.

"Optional?"

Everybody. Except Cole. He has to wear brown high-tops.

We were victorious in New Orleans 30–7, but it was not an impressive win. The offense was deeply involved in their patented Arthur Murray attack—one, two, three, *kick*— and the defense suffered accordingly. Our thirty points did not come in the calculated, time-consuming drives that Tom likes to see; instead we scored in flurries, and coasted—not the Cowboy style at all.

As anticipated, New Orleans was not our biggest problem in the game. It was the damn still air, searing heat, and withering humidity. My contact lenses fogged up in the first quarter and I never recovered.

As we jogged out for pregame warm-ups I developed a vague apprehension about the game. It was not the usual case of butterflies, but a shifting, gnawing uneasiness. I had experienced the same kind of feeling once before, on a used-car lot in California; it's the feeling that you are about to be flimflammed and there's nothing you can do about it. I couldn't logically connect the two situations and resolve my anxiety during calisthenics, so I let it ride.

In the middle of the third quarter I was lounging on the bench gazing into the sweaty Saturday-night crowd . . . and the feeling crystallized. There were 81,000 people in the stadium, an exhibition-game attendance record. I hastily estimated an average expenditure per fan, including concessions, of $8. This rapidly boiled down to over $600,000 in revenues. My share, according to the established NFL preseason pay scale, was $175. Both teams were paid off with less than $20,000.

August 21. Coach Landry addressed the squad this morning regarding the sloppiness of the New Orleans game and the obvious consequences of playing consistently inconsistent football.

"We are making too many mistakes for this stage of our preseason schedule," he said. "If we don't correct these errors now, they will manifold themselves during the regular season."

Unfortunately, Coach Landry is often guilty of language manipulation. It can be distracting if he is trying to make a legitimate point, but more often than not the outcome is at least humorous . . . particularly in the light of Tom's projected image as a precise, efficient, intelligent individual. In the first meeting of training camp Tom had delivered a carefully prepared speech to the defensive backs on the goals for the season. "This year," he concluded, "we'll be teaching and concentrating *so much* on techniques that when you get out there on the field . . . you'll be able to talk to each other . . . uh . . . in words."

Marshall McLuhan, the controversial communications expert, has observed that "a slip of the tongue gets more attention than an ordinary statement: thud and blunder." Herein lies the key to the hilarity and popularity of Tom's malapropisms, misnomers, and mispronunciations. In the stifling atmosphere of our infinite meetings, anything unexpected offers momentary relief and receives full attention.

Besides occasionally getting himself into a grammatical jam—and besides constantly mispronouncing the words "grasp," "crisp," "business," and "banana" *—Coach Landry has a problem with players' names. Admittedly a name like Kowalkowski would give a headache to a jackhammer operator. Tom's difficulties, however, are not quite so complex. Mike Montgomery was with the club for two weeks before Tom stopped referring to him as "Mc-Cormack." In the course of one film session Tom interrupted himself, turned from the projector, and with a puzzled frown asked, "Who's number 51?" There was dead silence, then an uproar. Number 51 was Dave Manders, the starting center, . . . and a Dallas Cowboy for nine years.

---

* "Banana" is the outstanding example. There is a pass pattern called "X-banana," which at first attempt becomes "X-bananal." If Tom has occasion to mention the route more than once, the metamorphosis is as follows: "bananal," . . . "banamo," . . . . "mananmo," . . . "forget it!!"

Opposing players pose just as much of a stumbling block. Among the football stars running around in Tom's mind are Mick Tinglehoffer, John Killiam, Buck Buckcannon, Fred Dyer, Jerry Philmore, John Brockingham, Gale Gilliam, Joe Scarpeter, . . . ad infinitum.

Blaine did not have a particularly outstanding game against New Orleans, and during the film session Coach Landry was not kind.

"Nye, for the last time, on an odd defense with no one over you, you're the pickup guy—you pick up for everybody. That's not too tough, is it, Nye?"

"Shit," Blaine whispered. "He's back to calling me Nye. In the third quarter he'll be calling me sixty-one."

Duane finally showed up in San Diego last week. He put on his sweat suit, went out to the practice field, exchanged greetings with Coach Svare, and then took it on in. Duane never has been a big proponent of the exhibition season.

The Jets and Joe Willie are in town this weekend, probably to atone for the 52–10 drubbing they suffered here last year. Bob Davis quarterbacked that game, but Namath is back this year, and anytime he steps on the field, the Jets are automatically trouble. He loves to throw, and his linemen love to protect. All he requires is one hot receiver and the opposing team is in for a long afternoon.

The Jet offensive line is superb at what has become their trademark—holding. They are the grabbingest sons-of-bitches in the league. Coach Ewbank has undoubtedly instructed his linemen to grab the defensive man rather than let him escape and get a shot at Joe. A fifteen-yard penalty can be tolerated; losing the entire Jet offense (and the biggest draw in the league) can not. So far this year, in three games Namath has not been touched.

Gil approached me today bearing . . . . tidings. "Pat, I'm trying to talk Tex into giving you some more money. It looks pretty good. We think you deserve it."

What could I say? I am currently in the final year of a three-year contract. I am playing for twenty thousand dollars plus two thousand additional if I am a "regular in the eyes of Coach Landry" for the duration of the season. I think I deserve a small raise myself. Gil called later that evening.

"Tell you what I'll do: I'm going to tack an additional five thousand on your starter's clause . . ."

"Great. Where do I sign?"

". . . if you sign a contract at twenty-seven thousand for the next year and thirty thousand for the following year."

"I'll think about it."

An injury during the season would wipe out that seven-thousand dollar bonus, and I would be locked in for three prime years at below-average pay. I'm going to gamble on staying healthy, having some decent years, and collecting on down the line.

Sid Gillman, bubbling with confidence since his recent elevation to on-the-field coaching duties, today posed his first question in a team meeting: "Now let me get this straight, Tom. If y is the prime receiver and the quarterback is keying the middle linebacker and the free safety, and if the middle linebacker and free safety go weak, does the quarterback then trraaannnnnnssffffeer his allegiance back to the tight end?"

Another verbal gymnast.

I dropped by Walt Garrison's room the morning of the Jet game and found him dutifully preparing for another gridiron battle. Walt was sitting comfortably against the headboard of his bed, hacking on a piece of basswood; a generous dip of Skoal protruded from his lower lip, and Tom T. Hall crooned from a portable tape deck.

"C'mon in," Walt said, spitting neatly into the trash can, "I'm waitin' on ol' Fluff Lane."

For the uninitiated, Skoal is the U. S. Tobacco Company's significant contribution to the satisfaction of America's need for oral gratification. It is a finely ground, blackberry-colored tobacco, tastefully flavored with just a dash of wintergreen. What you do is take a bit of snuff (a dip) between your thumb and forefinger and deftly place it in your mouth between cheek and gum—and there it sits, burning like hell, generating saliva. On the surface this dipping of snuff does not appear to be an alluring habit, but the rewards are considerable; the coefficient of pleasure and relaxation is comparable to that of the single cigarette following a bacchanalian feast.

"People who haven't tried it just don't understand," Walt claims. "Man, you get up in the morning . . . get a headful of that bullshit . . . oh, m' God, it's good!"

Just then Jerry ("Fluff") Lane rambled in, a guitar in his hand and a song in his throat (he had so much snuff in his mouth he couldn't sing). Lane is a serious songwriter in the country-and-western genre who has enjoyed a modicum of commercial success (Charley Pride, "Time You're Not a Friend of Mine"; Jack Greene, "The Hardest Easy Thing"). I didn't realize it, but he also has an unpublished lighter side—which he unveiled this morning.

"I've finally got it, Walt," Lane said, getting situated. "See what you think." He fingered a G-chord, composed himself, and began:

> If you think that love is the greatest of pleasure,
> If you think that gold is the greatest of treasure,
> If you think salvation will free your soul,
> Well, friend, you ain't had your first dip of Skoal!

Lane proceeded with "Asphalt It's Your Fault" and "Jesus Was a Baylor Bear." He closed with the classic rodeo love song "She Can Blow the Chrome Right Off My Trailer Hitch," and we went rollicking to the stadium.

We slipped by the Jets 34–27 in a sloppy, sluggish exhibition game. The Jets came out and acted as if they were going to blow us off the field. They led at the half by twenty points. At that point Namath retired from the game; we scored three quick ones in the final quarter, and eased away with a victory.

A torrential rain significantly tarnished the evening's performance. When the turf in Texas Stadium is wet, the footing goes. Receivers can't run their routes, ball carriers can't make their cuts, and linemen can't make their blocks. You've got twenty-two professional football players looking like a spastic group of Ice Capade dropouts. Traction becomes an obsession. On wet days some of our ballplayers will even remove their nylon cleats and play on the exposed metal posts.

The peculiar construction of Texas Stadium makes all this possible. For all intents and purposes, the stadium is domed. However, in the middle of the roof, directly over the playing field, is a two-and-a-half-acre hole. When it rains, snows, or sleets, it does so on the participants only.

"Hell," Charlie commented during the game, "if Clint"—owner Clint Murchison—"wanted us to fight the elements, why didn't he just roof the son-of-a-bitch over and put in a sprinkler system?"

Ironically, the gentlemen of the press voted Texas Stadium the finest facility in the NFL. Initially, I found that difficult to believe. Down in the player dressing rooms you'll find several lockers, several showers, a cooler of hot pop, and two (count 'em) tired toilets; the playing surface ranks next to the Astrodome's as the worst in the league. (One of the players' wives, on a tour of the facility with Tex Schramm, commented on the excessive firmness of the artificial turf. "It only feels hard when you walk on it," Tex replied.) I then visited the stadium press box.

The press box is plush. An elaborate buffet is set up before each game, replete with Texas barbecue, all the trimmings, and unlimited beer (hard stuff isn't served until after the game). A broadcast of the contest, with instant replay and no commercials, is piped into a series of Sony monitors, one for every pair of sportswriters. The dissemination of information (play-by-play, post-game quotes, etc.) is efficient; there are Texettes to make beer runs, and chairs comfortable enough to sleep in. When compared to other press boxes around the league, "It's the difference between the Dark Ages and the Renaissance," as Frank Luksa, of the Dallas *Times Herald,* said. "Undoubtedly the finest press facility in the land."

August 28. The weekly film sessions were enlightening, as usual. Tom mentioned that Namath, at $250,000 per year, is underpaid, and our defense, at (I'm guessing) $13,000 per man, was grossly overpaid. His point was that we had played badly, which was pretty obvious from the film. Tom linked our generally uninspired play to the fact that nobody wanted to stay after practice and work.

"If someone were just opening that door at the conclusion of practice," he said, "they would be trampled."

"They better widen that door," Lilly said as we filed out of the meeting room, "it's goddamn *hot* out there!"

The heat . . . I feel confident Dallas has more time and temperature signs per capita than any other city in the United States. Each of the electronic shrines offers a blow-by-blow description of the day's climbing thermometer. I've developed an unusual loathing for one in particular, the Bryant Heating and Cooling sign on North Central Expressway. As I drive by to the meetings every morning, the damn sign inevitably reports that it's 92 degrees—already.

We play Kansas City this week, Oakland next week, and then (at last) the season begins.

Three of our blossoming rookies were sampling the fare at the Holiday Inn's noon buffet when they were rudely interrupted: "WILL RICHARD AMMAN, MAURICE DAIGNEAU, AND CHUCK ZAPIEC PLEASE REPORT TO COACH LANDRY IN THE HOTEL LOBBY. IMMEDIATELY. THANK YOU." The Turk, wielding a savage blade, has trimmed the roster to forty-nine.

There was some wire-service news out of Miami today on Steve Kiner. He has reportedly decided to cut his hair and devote his full attention to the game of football. He also claims to have kicked a drug habit he had been cultivating for three years. "I'm ready for a clean start," Steve said.

Jethro Pugh, Larry Cole, George Andrie, and I passed the afternoon discussing the infinite subtleties of Tom Landry's flex defense. Most defensive linemen in the NFL play a penetrating "blow and go" style of defense. On the snap of the ball they take an all-out charge to the quarterback, and trust to their reactions if a running play develops; set responsibilities are kept to an absolute minimum. The flex defense is entirely different. It is a coordinated defense based on Tom's "gap theory." As a play develops, each man moves into a specific gap; every gap is accounted for, and the runner has no place to run. This defense has been very effective. One half of the line is aligned in a traditional "outside 4–3," a deployment common to most teams; the other side of the line is in the offset, or flex, position. The flexed side is predetermined according to the opposition's favorite formations, down and distance tendencies, etc. The flexed end is aligned head-up on the offensive tackle, one yard from the line of scrimmage, in a very awkward four-point stance. The adoption of this position makes it convenient for the knowledgeable fan to pick out the flexed side of the defense: he just locates the guy who looks like a crippled frog.

The flexed tackle lines up as close to the offensive guard's face as he can get. One of the obvious prerequisites for playing this position is tremendous quickness. It doesn't hurt either if, in addition, the ballplayer possesses a particularly pungent brand of concentration-breaking halitosis.

The defensive end, squatting there like a sick buffalo, does not even key the offensive tackle; instead, he peers in at the offensive guard for his clues. If the guard pulls, the end takes a six-inch step with his inside foot, meets the 280-pound tackle "tough" with his inside forearm, sheds the blocker (no sweat), and does a two-step shuffle into the vacated guard position. Meanwhile, the defensive tackle chases the guard around, hoping to get into the play. Now, if the guard doesn't pull . . .

"Goddamn ballet football," Tody Smith offered in passing.

"Shit, Pat, it's not that hard," George Andrie said, speaking from ten years' experience at defensive end. "You're keying that guard, right? You carefully take the first half of your six-inch step . . . that big tackle is thundering by now . . . you plant that inside foot, ... yell 'CRASH!!' and let Lilly slide out and make the play. I've made Bob All-Pro for years like that."

The Miami Dolphins gave Steve Kiner his unconditional release from football.

Charlie, Cliff, and Gene Stallings were standing around yesterday afternoon discussing the finer points of punting with Marvelous Marv Bateman. Bateman, a rookie, is battling Ron Widby for Ron's punting position. The format for the competition is standard; Widby will kick in one game, Bateman will perform in the next. Whoever is on top at the conclusion of the preseason will be our punter. The problem Bateman was discussing with Coach Stallings was who would kick to the return specialists during the week.

"The alternate kicker should kick," Marv suggested. "That way the guy who has to play that weekend isn't exhausted by game time."

"No, Marv," Gene said with a wink, "the rookie should kick *all* the time."

"Well, that's bullshit," Bateman said seriously.

Coach Stallings was shocked. "What'd you say, boy?"

"Well, . . . that's bullshit."

I bumped into Gene in the locker room and he told me about his confrontation with Bateman. We agreed that respect for your elders had become a relic.

"What's going on in the meeting room?" Gene asked as we headed out the door.

"Oh, just the players bitching about management."

"Goddawg," Gene said. "You ought to know that it's the management's neck on the line. Hell, if the club folded, the players wouldn't be out a thing. The owners are taking all the chances; they're entitled to a little edge."

Now, that's bullshit.

After fifteen straight victories we lost to Kansas City tonight 20–10. The shadow of disaster cast itself early; we concluded our pregame prayer with a thanks to the Lord for the cool weather and the fine crowd. We took the field with confidence and a lot of false chatter. On the third play of the game, one of their fat linemen rumbled the length of the field for six. The game deteriorated from there.

During the review of the Kansas City game films, John Niland was berated for his lack of second effort.

"John, you're only taking one shot at it," Tom lectured. "You've got to improve on your second effort."

Five minutes later: "John, it's a one-shot deal. You've got to come on now, there's no question about it."

Five minutes later: "Again," Tom strained, his voice rising, "you are only taking one shot at the man. We've got to
get you out of that habit."

A qualitative analysis of the meeting yielded some interesting results. Niland, who was once known as Gorgo, the
Frog that Ate the World, has now become Johnny One-
Shot. A direct relationship between Johnny One-Shot and
one of the fundamental rules of football was also revealed.

"Why are there thirty seconds between each offensive
play?" Larry Cole asked.

I didn't know for sure.

"So Niland can reload."

Billy Parks and Mike Montgomery, the former San
Diego Chargers who came to Dallas in the Thomas trade,
are finally settled in with miscellaneous wives, dogs, and
household goods. It has got to be difficult to pack up and
move on short notice. They wandered in to see Tex yesterday to collect their moving allowances, and Tex, in what is
becoming typical behavior, asked for receipts—to prove
they had moved.

As the deadline for cutting players draws nigh, some
interesting complications are developing. At quarterback
Craig Morton is solid as the starter. The number-two slot is
up for grabs, and the contenders are Iggy Concussion, as
Concannon is known to his friends, and Dan Reeves, the
offensive backfield coach who was shunted to the precari-
ous position of active player when Staubach was injured in
Los Angeles. The purpose of that whole affair seems to
have been to get Reeves off the coaching staff and Sid
Gillman out of the office and onto the field as his replace-
ment. With a cut approaching Wednesday, Reeves could
conceivably be through with football. If the worst does
happen, Dan, in the space of one month, will have un-
dergone a complete metamorphosis—from a "brilliant
young coach with an unlimited future" to a total reject. It

is difficult to understand. Most of the other players are watching the Reeves situation very closely; the feeling is that if the Cowboys go ahead and stick it to Reeves, no one is immune.

The incumbent kickers seem to be in trouble this cut also. Mike Clark is being severely pressured by strong-legged Toni Fritsch, and Ron Widby is sweating out rookie Marv Bateman. Something has got to give here, and the grapevine says it will be Widby and Clark.

Cliff Harris phoned last night at ten. His news was that Widby and Isaac Thomas had been traded to Green Bay for an undisclosed draft choice.

I was practically run down by Ike as I pulled into the Holiday Inn parking lot for this morning's meeting. He was going the other way. Apparently he was not informed of his new status until this morning.

A professional athlete doesn't get much sincere fan mail these days. Most of the time the correspondence is from some thirty-two-year-old kid with a mimeograph machine who majored in form letters. Sample:

Dear____ballplayer,
     You are my favorite____ballplayer. Could I please have your autograph? Enclosed please find a self-addressed, stamped envelope for your convenience.

Your fan,
John Giovininni
Bronx, N. Y. C.

The damn letters are always from somewhere in New York City, and they are never signed, just stamped in purple ink.

I have received one personal note this year—it came in yesterday's mail:

Dear Pat,

. . . I watch you every time you play. I like
your style, but I'm not really too smart when it
comes to judging ability . . .

Swell.

There was a short, stubby fellow out observing practice
today. He stalked the sidelines crisply, like an ex-marine
looking for his old unit on Armed Forces Day. Concannon
knew him.

"That was Ed Cody Ed Cody," Jack said.

"What?"

"Ed Cody Ed Cody—the coach who says everything
twice."

"Oh. He looked like a tough little son-of-a-bitch. . . ."

"My ass. That's just what he wants you to think. He's
like most coaches . . . insecure as hell." Concannon says
everything in a rich, Chicago-Boston-Irish-Italian-mobster
dialect. "We were sitting in a meeting one day, me and
Brian Piccolo, at Wrigley Field. They had those old, rusty,
card-table chairs . . . that only sit on three legs. Cody was
going through his shtick: 'All right, we got a South Mo
South Mo with a forty-nine toss . . . good play good
play.'"

In his fervor, Coach Cody forcefully drew up the South
Mo formation and exploded the chalk, sending chalk
shrapnel all over the room.

"The son-of-a-bitch bent over to pick up a fragment and
slammed his head into one of those rotten chairs." Jack
was snickering. "It put a tremendous gash in Ed's forehead, but he was tough. He refused to tend the wound.
When the blood started trickling off the end of his nose,
Piccolo and I couldn't stand it. We crawled out of the room
in hysterics."

Concannon had seen Cody during that off-season at a
golf tournament. It was a just-spring Chicago day—45 degrees and drizzling. Everyone was bundled up in sweaters

and heavy rain gear. Everyone except Cody. Ed had on some Bermuda shorts and a windbreaker. The Bermudas exposed a fresh, six-inch, gently curving scar on his right knee. Cody spotted Concannon.

"How ya doin' how ya doin'?" Ed said.

"What in the hell happened to you?" Jack asked, staring at Cody's knee, picturing a diving save in some handball game.

"Oh that," Ed said modestly. "You're not going to believe it."

"You reenlisted."

"Naw. I was down at the car wash . . . I climbed out of the car and watched it disappear into the spray . . . all that spray. Next thing I knew, I was jerked on my back . . . down on my back. The goddamn chain thing had me by the pants leg and was dragging me through the goddamn car wash. I got all the way to Spray Wax before they shut the son-of-a-bitch off. It tore up my knee pretty good . . . pretty goddamn good."

In our continuing effort to get down to the forty-man squad, Mike Clark and Claxton Welch were released, and Don Talbert and Brian Goodman were placed on the taxi squad. Mike had been with the Cowboys for four or five years and had performed admirably. Sometime last year it occurred to Tom that Clark was not the ultimate kicker (in the first place, Mike is an American). The ultimate team must have the ultimate kicker, so Tom dispatched Gil Brandt, who dispatched Bob Kapp into the soccer hinterlands. Kapp returned with Herr Fritsch, and it was just a matter of time before Clark was sent packing.

Clark and Fritsch alternated kicking assignments through most of the exhibition season. In the most recent game—Clark's last game—Toni lost track of the rotation and went out to kick off on Mike's turn. Clark was sent out to take his proper turn, and was practically booed to the sidelines. Classic fan sensitivity.

Unfortunately, more people must be cut. There is an especially large logjam at the wide-receiver position, where a couple of good rookies—Robert West and Charles McKee—are competing with veterans Bob Hayes, Lance Alworth, Ron Sellers, and Billy Parks. Lance is concerned. He has caught only one pass this season, for a total of seven yards.

The turnover is nearly 40 percent this year, and we were a World Championship club six months ago.

We play the Oakland Raiders Saturday night and the excitement in our camp is unparalleled. Somebody asked Cliff if the team was up for the game. He thought for a while. "The only other place I have experienced this kind of excitement . . . was on a seven-forty-A.M. commuter out of Trenton, New Jersey."

Coach Landry was discussing today the general potential of his defensive philosophy if properly understood and executed. The success of the flex defense depends entirely on the absolute coordination of all eleven men. Each man must take his key on the snap of the ball and execute his assignment.

"If all eleven men are moving and reacting as a unit," Tom explained, "the flex defense can stop any great running team or any great individual runner."

It logically follows that the defensive unit's preparation for a game is geared to studying the opponent's offensive tendencies. A computer printout of that pertinent information is furnished each week for study purposes.

"Won't our opponents change their thinking when they are faced with the flex defense?"

"Good teams don't change," Tom replied. "I don't worry about 'what if' out there; I worry about 'what is.' You can draw up plays from now until the Super Bowl that may be effective against the flex. However, unless a team has been running that play week in and week out, they will not be able to execute effectively against you. If they are running some crazy plays on you, we'll pick it up on the sidelines and make the necessary adjustments."

"That's a laugh," whispered George. "The only time they spot anything unusual is in the game films . . . on Monday."

We are down to forty active players once again. They have cut West and McKee from the receiver corps, and Brian Goodman from the offensive line. Goodman had been shifted to the taxi squad in the aftermath of last week's cutdown. He looked to be in a good position to sneak on the roster and collect some of that big money but Coach Landry decided to keep Talbert.

The last guy to go was Lee Roy Caffey. Caffey was in the twilight of his career, trying to hang on for just one more year—and he almost made it. The Cowboys had put him through waivers several weeks ago, and the St. Louis Cardinals claimed him. Then the Cowboys withdrew his name. Now they have cut him again, in the final cut, a no-recall situation. By this time in the year most clubs have set their rosters and are not interested in any latecomers from other teams. Unless Lee Roy has a powerful friend, in all probability he'll be heading home to south Texas.

Wednesday, September 13. Coach Landry delivered his annual "Amateur Drawing Pay" speech this morning. His timing is typical; we are four days from our league opener, and we are coming off of a ragged performance against Oakland. The gist of the lecture was this: A *PRO* doesn't worry about coaches or situations; he knows what he must do and he does it. Some of us are *PROS*, . . . and some of us are just AMATEURS DRAWING PAY." It was a very inspirational talk.

Tom also explained that the traditional forty-man squad

was obsolete, and as of this year, we will have a new tradition—the forty-seven-man squad. Every man will be on
full salary; hence there will be no official taxi squad. The
composition of the inactive group will be subject to
change according to injuries, performance, etc.

This innovative concept seems to be a neat package of
protection for the Cowboys and their unproductive high-
draft choices. Tody Smith (number one) and Ike Thomas
(number two) have not measured up to expectations; they
have done nothing (Ike has already been traded). To keep
such individuals on the active roster would be ludicrous,
as they are in no position to help the club. To negotiate a
(drastically reduced) taxi-squad contract, they would have
to first clear waivers. This would never happen. The solution is to pay everybody full salary—hence the forty-seven-
man-squad concept—and frost the situation by claiming
that "all of our players are able to contribute; therefore we
cannot justify a cab squad on the 'players of the future'
basis."

Philadelphia this weekend. Wade Key is my tackle for
the game. He is not exactly a household name, but then
neither am I. We ought to be a good match-up. The Eagles
are notoriously wild, infused with some mysterious super-
natural chemical that induces hyperactivity. When you
play them you've got to have your head on a swivel; they
are masters of the unexpected cheap shot.

Steve Kiner was cut today from the Washington Redskins. Simultaneously, Duane Thomas told Harland Svare
in San Diego that he would probably sit out the season.
The dynamic duo is out of football after two years.

Forrest Gregg, of the San Diego Chargers, phoned Lee
Roy Caffey yesterday and asked him to come out and join

the club. Harland Svare is surrounding himself with what he interprets as the remains of the Lombardi magic. Forrest is his offensive line coach, Willie Wood is there in some capacity, Phil Bengston is the personnel director, and now Caffey is going to play middle linebacker.

Coach Landry experimented along those same lines last year. We had Forrest, Lee Roy, and Herb Adderley from the Packer championship clubs. What Tom discovered was that the Lombardi magic worked fine . . . for Lombardi and his highly motivated crew of seven years ago, but an over-the-hill Packer today has nothing to offer but his rapidly deteriorating physical ability. Lee Roy and Forrest lasted but one season in Dallas.

Saturday-morning practices are the highlight of my football week. The equipment manager lays out a doughnut banquet, there's coffee or milk or drink, and everybody's nine-year-old is running amok. The meeting is blissfully short. We go out in sweat suits, throw each other passes, and generally feel like our kids.

We beat Philadelphia 28–6 in the league opener. As Eagle–Cowboy games go, this one was typical; the Eagles gave us fits. At half time the score was 7–6 and neither team was moving particularly well. "Movement," of course, is one of those vague football terms which apply to the winning team, and sportswriters seem to accept it as an explanation for the outcome of a game: "They were just moving a lot better than we were. . . ." At any rate, we came out for the second half, started moving better offensively, and pulled away.

On one particular play, a slant hand-off to my side, Wade Key and I were stalemated on the line of scrimmage. The ballcarrier turned upfield, looking for the seam between Lilly and myself. I tried to push Key into the hole. As I did, Lilly, who had come off his block, threw himself into the hole and crashed perfectly into Key's knee. Key screamed and melted into the turf. The rest of us felt a little sick.

Ernie Calloway, a large, young defensive lineman for the Eagles, stumbled into old acquaintance Blaine Nye in Palo Alto during the off-season. Blaine asked Ernie how things were progressing and Ernie implied that things weren't going that well.

"... in fact," he muttered, "I'm thinking about retiring."

Blaine was confused. "Hell, Ernie," he said, "you're a young guy; you must have five or six years left. What's the problem?"

"I'll tell you," Ernie replied. "When I came into this league, I was even with the world. . . . I didn't owe nobody nothing'. After my first year, I was five thousand dollars in debt; after my second year, I was ten thousand dollars in the hole; and now, this year, I'm twenty-four thousand dollars down. . . . SHIT!! I can't afford to play anymore!"

Coach Landry was disappointed with our performance in the opening game. Specifically—he thought we were not ready to hit, he thought we looked sluggish out there, and he thought we were not sufficiently warmed up when the game started (Hayes pulled a muscle in the first quarter). When a team has problems of this magnitude, prompt action by the head coach is essential to head off a total collapse. After all, we had lost to Philly in a disastrous opener—or had we? I was under the distinct impression that we had won the game 28–6.

"From now on," Coach Landry began in a remedial way, "we will wear our shoulder pads for pregame warm-up so we'll be ready to hit. From now on, no one will be allowed to drink Cokes before the game or at half time . . . they make you logy. From now on, there will be supervised stretching exercises in the locker room to loosen up before we got out to loosen up."

Ah . . . warming up for the warm-ups. We did lose the game.

Apparently Tom was convinced our sluggishness was due to something we had eaten; he came down hard on our pregame meal. "That steak you guys have been eating stays with you the entire game. When I have food on my stomach, it adversely affects my coaching performance. That's why I eat oatmeal for the pregame meal." Hint, hint. Tom totally ignored the fact that the temperature on the field was over 100, and the humidity was in excess of 80 percent. "The heat," Tom decreed, "is entirely mental. When you pass out, it becomes physical."

The preparation for the New York game commenced today, and Tom joined us for the second half of the meeting. The point he was intent on hammering in, this morning, was that New York is much improved over last year, and in order to win, we've got to stop Ron Johnson and Bob Tucker (Ernie had earlier referred to them as "Red Category" players: super). Coach Landry, having played and coached in New York for a number of years, has some interesting insights into the Giant offensive philosophy. "The New York Giants have a knack for sneaking. It's the way they do things," he explained, "and they've done it for as long as I can remember. Morrison, Gifford when they had him, these were guys who knew how to look— and then sneak." Our defensive game plan will probably entail wearing tennis shoes and making as little noise as possible.

The Cowboys' one-man Research and Development department, Ermal Allen, makes up the weekly personnel reports and will frequently interject some of the enlightening opinions he has formulated during his research. For instance, in the New Orleans scouting report he had surmised that

Carlos Bell . . . will drop the ball in the clutch. . . .
Joe Williams . . . has hands of steel. . . .
Archie Manning . . . has the guts of a burglar.

He had a fascinating statistic on Norm Snead this week:

> Norm Snead . . . has thrown more interceptions
> than touchdowns in ten years of competition.

"Remember," Jim Myers cautioned the offensive line, "indecision will never consistently get the job done."

Saturday morning in New York. Reeves usually combines the roll call with a menu check for the pregame meal. Everyone ordered oatmeal!

Tom dusted off his perennial New York pregame speech this morning, and it hasn't changed much over the years. He usually praises the city as the place where professional football as we know it originated, and he always emphasizes the importance of New York as a media center. One year he even mentioned that he knew of players who had made All-Pro by virtue of one outstanding performance in Gotham City. I can never decide whether he is extolling the power of the media, or pointing out the absurdity sometimes involved in making All-Pro.

The perennial New York pep talk had its perennial effect: we had a hell of a time beating the Giants. The final score was 23–14, but the game was even tighter than the score suggests. The Giants were as sneaky as their advance notices indicated, and we had problems coping. They are fond of lining up in strange formations (e.g., tight end in the backfield, halfback at wide receiver), and sending these out-of-position players into motion as the quarterback calls the snap count. Instead of playing a basic defense, we reacted to their weird formations and odd sets with complications of our own. We tried to adjust to every wrinkle, and the net result was confusion.

Herb Adderley did not enjoy a good game against the Giants, and there is reason to believe Coach Landry is grooming Charlie Waters for the left-cornerback position. Tom has had little to say to Herb this year, other than to berate him for his play; Charlie, on the other hand, has been the object of increasing attention. A take-over is imminent. Admittedly, Herb is getting on in years, but he was a vital cog during the Super Bowl seasons, a key to the Cowboys' success. The situation calls for at least a spark of respect from the coaching staff, but apparently that's too much to ask.

The Monday meeting and film sessions generally reflect Tom's attitude toward the just-completed game, and his views on what we've got to do to improve. This week we did not play with enough emotion. "We're not playing with enough emotion," Tom said, and proceeded to present the game balls a la George Allen. Standard practice is to present game balls immediately following the game. Everybody says, "Hey hey hey," and it's done with. Today Tom came up with a production number. He gave each selected player a mountainous buildup, and then, as the finale, rifled the ball across the room to where the particular player was sitting. One had to be on the alert. . . . Tom has a rag arm.

Coach Landry was obviously uncomfortable in his new role. "My God," I thought, "we have created a monster." But no, when the lights went out and the film started to roll, Tom reverted to his old self.

"You know, professional football is funny," Blaine commented on coming out of the meeting. "It's not whether you win or lose, . . . it's who gets the blame."

"That is the worst Tom has graded on grading me," Cole added.

Jethro Pugh was the only player who merited any praise at all. Tom congratulated him on having "six attackles and three assists."

We've got Green Bay tomorrow and there is some cause for concern; the Packers have some momentum going for them and we will be without our injured punter, Marvelous Marv Bateman. The punting sweepstakes, to determine who will take over the punting chores, are now in progress. Toni Fritsch will be our last resort. If no one else can punt, Toni will line up in field-goal position and try to kick the ball out of bounds. Oh my.

"One thing I like about football," Ralph Neely muttered, "there's always something new to panic about."

Their quarterback is Scott Hunter, a third-year man from Alabama. The last time I competed against Scott was back in college. The Commodores met the Alabama Crimson Tide on the plains of Dudley Field, in Nashville. The Tide carried a 3–0 record and a national ranking at the time; we were 0–3 and hadn't beaten Alabama since the mid-fifties. As we trotted onto the field for introductions, I gazed hopefully into our hometown throng. It could have been an Alabama home game: the crowd was dressed in red—and booing.

Shockingly enough, we won the game, 14–10. The clinching touchdown came on a perfectly executed, last-ditch, eighty-yard drive deftly engineered by a B-team center with a good arm, ("West End") Denny Painter. "This is the lowest point in Alabama history," Bear told the press after the game, and he was right.

The key to that victory was good pressure on Hunter. The week before, against Mississippi, he had been allowed to throw unmolested, and completed close to thirty passes. The Commodores knocked him around a bit, and Scott was able to manage only three completions in twenty-four attempts. A little dose of the same tomorrow could insure our success.

Dan Devine, the current Packer mentor and former Missouri fanatic (he reportedly named his son "Tige," after the Missouri Tigers), has installed a half-roll, scramble-blocking, college attack with two pros carrying the mail— John Brockington and MacArthur Lane. Devine is also utilizing a dose of NCAA psychology. He was whining today about the ineffectiveness of Hunter, the potentialities of

backup quarterback Jerry Tagge, and the "crucial" injuries
to All-Pro Gale Gillingham and Francis Peay. I feel Devine is attempting to lull us to sleep.

It worked. We lost 16–13 in what is becoming the Dallas
Cowboys' annual giveaway; we had five or six turnovers, a
plethora of mental errors, and occasional pandemonium on
the sidelines. We lost precisely in this manner to New
Orleans and Chicago last season. Billy Clyde Puckett has
stated that you shouldn't never lose to the dog-asses of the
league . . . and he's right. But I have a feeling that this
year Green Bay is no dog-ass.

My opponent for this game was Bill Hayhoe. Six-foot-
eight, 275-pound Bill Hayhoe. Hi ho with Hayhoe. Actually Bill was not a bad sort of fellow. On one particular
play the Green Bay offense broke the huddle and lined up
in an I formation (two backs in the backfield, one directly
behind the other). My assignment for the I formation was
to crash through the offensive tackle's shoulder on the
snap of the ball and generally work havoc in their backfield. This is an excellent tactic if the tackle is pulling out,
blocking down on Lilly, or otherwise vacating the area
where I am going to be. On this play, however, he fired directly out at me, and POOM . . . maximum impact on
collision. He caught me right in the chest. I felt myself
being lifted up. Obviously, the tight end could not resist
such a vulnerable target. I felt myself airborne . . . going
over . . . on my back. When I opened my eyes Hayhoe
was on top of me, breathing into my face. I surmised that
Hayhoe had had beer and pizza the night before. Needless
to say, this is a very frustrating position for a defensive
lineman to be in, particularly if he wants to be a football
star.

"Christ," Hayhoe chuckled, "we don't even have that
play in our offense!"

"Ha ha," I replied, and we proceeded back to our respective huddles.

Hi ho with Hayhoe.

Coach Landry was not pleased with the loss. His post-game remarks dealt with a premonition he had prior to the game: "I could tell in pregame warm-up that the Packers were ready to go out there and play good football and we were flat . . . on our way to a poor game." Probably so, but why tell us afterward? A well-timed tirade before the game might have shaken us up and saved us from the clutches of defeat. But that's Tom; he believes his job has very little to do with motivating players. "If a pro can't motivate himself, fully realizing everything he has at stake, then he shouldn't be in this bidness."

The inherent flaw in Tom's nonmotivational psychology was in evidence Sunday. There are times when our team, as a collective whole, loses track of itself and requires some impetus, some point of focus, to get back on the right road. Sunday was one of those days. We didn't have it, Tom didn't give it to us, and we subsequently looked the fool.

The Washington Redskins, our bitter rivals in the quest for the Eastern Division title, did us a favor by dropping one yesterday also. Sportswriter Bob St. John asked Tom what he thought of Washington's defeat. "I never think about what Washington does," Tom lied.

I took a shot to the knee during the third quarter of the Green Bay contest. I planted my left leg, to attempt to hit on Brockington, and the pulling guard slammed into it. I limped off, had the knee taped up, and limped back on. It didn't really start aching until today.

The adrenalin and nervous energy generated during a game will often neutralize the pain of a noncritical injury incurred in the action. Finishing a game in which you have broken a small bone in your hand, for instance, or mildly sprained your ankle or knee, is relatively simple. The true test will come the following week, when you go *into* a game already hurt. Questions arise. The coaching staff wonders whether or not you can ignore your injury for two hours and adequately perform your job. You begin to wonder too. There are six days to think about it. A corollary to that question—one that depends on the nature of your injury and your status with the club—is, Can you *practice* with pain? If you want to, or if you feel you have to, there are ways.

I ventured out to practice today (Thursday, defensive day) well fortified with Empirin 3, a codeine-aspirin compound, and a heavy-duty tape job. No sweat. The decision to go ahead and practice was more or less determined by my status with the club. The preparation for the upcoming game is critical, of course, but game preparation is 90 percent mental. The physical act of practicing is therefore desirable, but not essential.

My problem is that I do not want to place my job (defensive end) in any undue jeopardy. I was a sixth-round draft choice and I made the team. I wasn't really expected to make it. Tody Smith is a defensive end and a number-one draft choice. As a number-one, he is expected to play, and to play well. Currently, he is playing behind Larry Cole and myself . . . if I am hurt and not occupying my position, Tody is there. With a good game or two, he will be there permanently. For that reason, I must play. I can't even afford to let him get comfortable out in practice.

The tension and frustration bred by the Green Bay loss surfaced today in our pass-rush drill. The drill is normally a docile event, but today there were flying forearms and . . . head slaps, of all things. Ernie Stautner and Jim Myers had words. Bob Lilly got upset.

"We've been pussified," he said. "I didn't notice it until today, by God, but we're in a pussified state! They hold—and we laugh. They hold and we laugh. Damn it all! From now on out, I'm taking my licks! I don't give a shit!"

By tomorrow, Bob should be back to his former self.

Thursday, October 5. Pittsburgh this week. Blaine has the fortuitous opportunity to manhandle Mean Joe Greene. If an offensive lineman has a good game against a player of Greene's caliber, people begin to notice; recognition around the league follows, and if you're lucky, maybe even a bid to the Pro Bowl. Blaine's own comments have run something like this:

> INTERVIEWER: Blaine, you're matched this week with Joe Greene of the Pittsburgh Steelers—
> BLAINE: Yes, we're matched all right; his strengths coincide exactly with my weaknesses.
> INTERVIEWER: Mean Greene is reputedly one of the strongest and most active defensive tackles in the NFL today. You *must* feel that added excitement that comes when you compete against the very best.
> BLAINE: I'm a little nervous, yes.
> INTERVIEWER: You're a pro, Blaine. I'm sure you would prefer to play against the best every week.
> BLAINE: Actually—I'd rather play a dog any day.

Our defensive backfield coach, Gene Stallings, journeyed up here to Dallas, the double-knit capital of the world, from the rather khaki environs of Texas A. & M. The reawakening of Gene's fashion consciousness has been interesting to behold. Upon his arrival, Gene set out to refurbish his wardrobe. He bought wild print shirts by the dozen, and geometric-design double-knit britches by the trunkload. Yesterday it all came together: devastatingly opposing stripes, clashing geometrics, a white belt, and a pair of extinct, black, 1964 alligator brogans. Gene was vibrant. Literally. You couldn't focus on him.

We beat Pittsburgh in a sloppy affair, setting our record at 3–1. We were 3–1 last year at this time, playing the same kind of error-plagued football. Our pattern of play over the past two years has been to start slow and finish strong. We've been in the Super Bowl both years. We're starting slow again this year; . . . I'm just hoping we have the ending down as well as we have the beginning.

The other day Danny Reeves was talking about Otto Brown, a former Cowboy cornerback now employed by the New York Giants. Just before the third game of Otto's rookie year, the equipment man, Jack Eskridge, was making the last call for Will Call tickets. "Any more tickets for Will Call!" Esky habitually screamed. "You got any tickets for Will Call, Brown?!" Esky shouted as he stormed by.

Otto shook his head and turned up to Reeves. "That Will Call is some rich dude, man. He's been to every game since I've been here!"

Otto once got a fan letter addressed to "Auto" Brown.

Our jolting, oblique touchdown at Friendship International Airport, Baltimore, relocated my entire digestive tract somewhere in the neighborhood of my tonsils. A rough landing always sparks a discussion of the inevitability of an NFL charter plane going down, and the conversation invariably leads back to December 14, 1968—a day of near disaster.

The Cowboys had whipped New York that Sunday, clinching their third division title and their fourth consecutive play-off appearance. By the time the team arrived at the airport to board the flight back to Dallas, a full-scale blizzard was in progress. The natural high of a successfully completed season was compounded and multiplied by the consumption of unlimited cases of beer. The two-hour wait on the end of the runway seemed short. The plane was cleared for takeoff. The aircraft struggled down the runway and lurched into the murk—and there was an explosion somewhere. The nose of the 727 was hopefully pointed skyward; however, the plane was locked in at an altitude of seventy-five feet. A stewardess came tumbling out of first class; hundreds of empty beer cans flew south to the butt of the plane.

Bob Lilly—half drunk, his eyes glazed—quickly assessed the situation. "THAT'S IT, BABY!" Bob hollered as he staggered from his seat and faced the rest of the cabin. "IT'S ALL OVER!" He too plummeted to the rear of the plane.

There was another muffled explosion. George Andrie and Chuck Howley were doing Hail Marys. D. D. Lewis didn't know what in the hell to do; he turned desperately to Don Meredith. Don was sitting in the window seat, arms folded, whistling.

"GODDAMN, GODDAMN!" D. D. screamed. "AREN'T YOU SCARED?!"

Meredith turned slowly. "Naw, D. D.," he drawled, "it's been a good 'un."

We shut down Baltimore 21–0. They have lost whatever they had that thrust them into the 1971 Super Bowl. The decay of a franchise usually shows up in its inability to draft college talent effectively. The top picks disappear in a year or so instead of developing into the steady players they were counted on to become. A second indicator is the quarterback. Johnny U. is practically forty years old and he just doesn't have the steam on the ball he once had. In preparing for the Colts in Super Bowl V, Ermal Allen charted Unitas' passing tendencies (whom he liked to throw to, from which hash mark, at what down and distance, and so on). What he discovered was that during the regular season Unitas threw very few sideline patterns. Ermal concluded that his arm was gone. That was a couple of years ago, and Unitas is still hanging on. Someone asked Unitas this year why he hadn't quit when he was the best quarterback in the league. "At a hundred and twenty-five thousand a year," he answered, "I can't afford to."

In the fourth quarter of the game, Unitas threw for the tight end in the end zone. Charlie Waters, substituting for Herb Adderley, closed fast on the down-and-in pattern, and Cliff came hard to help out. The ball bounced off tight end Mitchell incomplete; Charlie and Cliff collided head to head. Charlie, being the more sensitive of the two, was out stone cold. While the trainers were tending Charlie, Cliff somehow stumbled off the field and flopped down next to me. He leaned back on the bench, and encountering no support, went right on over. Though he artfully recovered by doing a backward somersault, he still had that glazed look in his eye. By this time the trainers had set Charlie down beside Cliff. Dr. Knight was with Charlie, talking to him, stuffing smelling salts up his nose.

"Okay, okay, . . . I think he's okay," the Doc said to the trainers. "CLIFF!!" He grabbed Cliff. "Cliff! Ask Charlie his assignments."

"Where am I?" Cliff responded . . . and keeled over.

Pregame. I was lounging around the locker room with Blaine and Larry when Robert Lilly wandered over and asked if anyone had a quarter. Robert's question was a bit peculiar since there is nothing to purchase in a stadium locker room.

"What have you got in mind, Bob?" Larry asked.

"Well," Bob said, "I've got it figured. We'll flip the quarter ten times and count the number of heads and tails. Whichever side shows most, we'll call in the official toss."

"Uh, Bob—" Blaine started an explanation, thought better of it, and gave Bob the quarter.

Post-game. Ralph Neely was ensconced in the back of the players' bus with his customary bottle of wine. D. D. Lewis wandered back for a taste.

"Hmmm . . . great!" he said. "What year is that?"

Ralph glanced at the bottle. "Vintage 1968."

D. D. shook his head. " 'Sixty-eight was a good year," he said. "I was supposed to graduate in 1968."

D. D. persevered and finally made it through school in 1972. Margaret, his wife, had intended to throw a graduation party for D. D. ". . . but after I thought about it," she said, "I was too embarrassed."

With the advent of George Allen in Washington, the Redskins have become formidable adversaries of the Cowboys. The standard problems encountered in preparing for any NFL team are compounded by the psychological perturbations that diffuse through the organization as a Washington game approaches. The source seems to be Coach Landry himself.

From what I can surmise, Tom views each Dallas–Washington contest as a fundamental philosophical confrontation: Landry, the clean-living, calculating strategist and overlord of the Eastern Division, versus George Allen, the clean-living, dirty-dealing newcomer and noted motivator of players.

The Allen–Landry rivalry was initiated some years ago in Thousand Oaks when Allen was with the Rams. The Cowboys swore that the Rams were filming Dallas practice sessions from atop a nearby hill. The treachery was discovered to have spread to Dallas County when Cowboy officials traced the license-plate number of a fleeing spy to a Los Angeles scout.

Whether George has done any espionage work within the past several years is unknown, but the Cowboy paranoia persists. Whenever we play Washington, the Cowboy collective mind is altered. In 1972 Tom went so far as to scramble practice times and change the practice location; we transferred to the Cotton Bowl, where security could be stepped up, and started practice thirty minutes later than usual.

We arrived at the Cotton Bowl one day, and in accordance with the new routine, the gates were locked behind us. Gil Brandt and Bob Griffin were already patrolling the upper reaches of the stadium, searching for incriminating evidence. Nothing there. Approximately twenty minutes into practice, I heard the muffled, machine-gun racket of a large helicopter. It was not yet in view, but it seemed to be circling the stadium. Finally the 'copter settled in at an altitude of about two hundred feet, just off the open end of the Cotton Bowl. It sat there for fifteen minutes.

I couldn't help laughing. We were all laughing—well, snickering really—because of the gravity of the situation. The coaches were trying hard to ignore the intruder, but the task was difficult. Ernie finally broke: "Fuck the Goddamn helicopter! Fuck it! We don't care what Allen knows about us. . . . We're going to whip his ass!!"

This week's preparation began on a humorous note. Coach Landry was lecturing the wide receivers on the cornerback play of Pat Fischer.

"As you know, Fischer likes to dog," Tom commented. "He gets right in your face and tries to stay with you step for step; he's quick, and he has a good nose for the football. Now Bobby, when Fischer starts his carousement tech . . ." Tom scratched his head. " 'Carousement?' Where in the heck did I get 'carousement'?"

"Harassment, coach."

"Oh, yes."

So it goes.

Cliff is in an uproar over Charley Taylor. Oddly enough, Taylor's pass-catching ability is not the cause of Cliff's concern; it's his blocking methods on running plays. Taylor glides toward the middle on a running play, searching for an unsuspecting safety. He approaches his target at three-quarter speed and sets to deliver a blow. Instead of utilizing the traditional cut-block technique most receivers use, he attempts to jam his forearm into the craw of the oncoming defensive back. The results are often horribly spectacular. In one game, against St. Louis, he managed to take Larry Wilson out for the afternoon, and to shatter Jerry Stovall's jaw, knocking him out for the season. The shortcoming of Taylor's unnecessary excesses is the inevitable retaliation that will follow. Defensive backs around the league are now looking for Taylor. His efficiency over the middle has already started to drop. . . . It's just a matter of time.

The Skins whipped us 24–20 at R.F.K. Stadium in Washington. We had them in trouble early, at one point 20–7, but we couldn't salt them away. Our defense broke down in the second half, Jurgensen went to work, and we won ourselves a long plane ride home.

Cliff came out on the short end of his duel with Taylor. The particular play was away from him, to our left; my angle of pursuit took me diagonally through our secondary. Cliff was in front of me, moving at full tilt, eyes riveted to the ballcarrier. The referee, trying to stay clear of the action, stepped right into Cliff's line. Cliff juked to avoid the official, and ran right into Taylor's well-placed forearm. Charley had been hiding behind the referee. Cliff got up, eyes watering, and cursed the official until he had exhausted his vocabulary.

After two hours of sweating and groveling in the dirt, we got no hot water for our showers. George doesn't miss a trick.

We had two days to mull the outcome before reporting for our weekly film session. My attitude was one of tempered resignation: we had blown the game, but Detroit was coming up, in a must-win situation. We'd have to correct our mistakes and get on with the task at hand. I was to discover immediately that this Washington defeat was much more than a number in the loss column.

Tom came into the meeting, jaw set and eyes piercing . . . cold. He skimmed over his usual evaluations and launched into an emotional sermon. The night after the game, he said, he went home and was preparing to retire. As most everybody does, he emptied his pockets, and for the first time, he removed his Championship ring. When he arose in the morning, he could not find it within himself to put the ring back on. "We did not play like champions," he said. Tom was not concerned with coping with any reaction to his talk, or with the nature of our loss. He classified anyone with anything to say as either a chronic complainer, a prima donna, or a weak sister. "Our team," Tom said, "is being undermined by these people."

George Allen is eroding Tom's psyche.

We finally got on the field for practice today at 3:30 P.M.

"You know what we are?" Dave ("Fuzzy") Edwards asked.

"What?"

"All-day suckers."

There were some "Other" awards presented today in the aftermath of our most recent disaster. The "Others," or "Extras" as they are often called, are all those players who are not starters. The function of the Others derives directly from the function of the college B team: "All right, we're going to go over the blitzes now. All you others come over here and give me an offense."

To qualify for an other award, you must enter the fray for one play—and lose the game. Charlie ("Sawdust") Waters and ("Hot") Rod Wallace are the designated co-captains, and, in informal ceremonies, presented two awards. The Super Remnant Award went to George Andrie. Big-play Andrie entered the game with Washington in possession on our twelve-yard line; they scored around right end on the very next play. The runner-up for the Super Remnant Award was offensive tackle Rodney Wallace. He entered the game in a crucial passing situation . . . and his man trapped the quarterback. Dutchess Montgomery received the Other of the Week Award (for the one who plays least and does worst); Monty has carried the ball three times this season and has yet to gain a yard.

Chuck Howley stormed into the field house one day last week incredibly upset at a radio station. KLIF in Dallas runs a morning talk session where no subject is taboo. It goes without saying that sex and the accompanying hang-ups are the principal topics of conversation.

A lady called in and announced that she was in need of a lesson in dream interpretation. The moderator asked what the dream was. He shouldn't have. The lady had dreamed that she was "laid" by Chuck Howley on the fifty-yard line at Texas Stadium . . . in front of sixty thousand people. Chuck was indignant. His wife had heard about the episode through one of Chuck's business clients. Chuck was pondering an immediate call to his attorney.

"I don't know what you're so pissed off about," Dave Manders said, breaking the silence. "It wasn't even a full house!"

The player telephone rang and Charlie Waters answered.

"Is Mr. Tuff there?" the voice on the line asked.

"Pardon me?"

"Mr. Tuff. Is Mr. Tuff there?"

"Would you spell that for me, please?"

"Sure. *T-u-g-h*."

"A-ha. You mean *P-u-g-h*."

"Ooooooooohhhhhhhhh, . . . yeah, man, . . . no wonder. . . . Well, look here, . . . is Mr. Puff there, man?"

In the continuing effort to stay abreast of Tom's forever-changing, multifaceted offense, Walt takes down every little change in his trusty notebook. Garrison feels he must write things down to aid his memory. On the other hand, Calvin Hill is a little haphazard in his bookkeeping, and Robert Newhouse keeps no book at all. Sid Gillman noticed the disparity in study habits and ordered a change. "Men, I'm tired of all the bullshit. If your notebooks aren't as neat as Walt's by this time next week, it's a fifty-dollar fine."

Walt did not relish the attention. "Shit," he said. "I'd rather have the clap than have Sid."

"What?"

"I know how to get rid of the clap."

There was a profile of Ernie Stautner in the printed program for the Monday-night Detroit game. Don Meredith dropped by the locker room before the game, heard us questioning Ernie's alleged viciousness, and offered the following as evidence:

"We were playing Pittsburgh, boys. It was second and six on our own forty-six early in the third quarter. I took the snap from center, faded back a bit, set, pumped, faded back a little more, and dropped a perfect screen pass right over little Ernie's head. It must have upset him. On the following down, I threw an out pattern and was standing around thinking about the next play when . . . *pow* . . . somebody belted me a good one from behind. I flew through the air, landed on my back, and lost my breath. Ernie sauntered over, casually stepped up on my chest, and stared into my helmet. 'If you ever try to throw another screen pass by me,' Ernie said calmly, 'you'll never play football again.'"

"Did you?"

"Hell no!"

Another year, the Cowboys were getting ready to play Pitt and the pass-rush drill was just getting under way. In the Wednesday drill, the defensive men try to provide practice for the offensive players by taking on the roles of

their upcoming opponents. George Andrie addressed of-
fensive-lineman Bob Fry:

"What kind of moves you want this week?"

"None," Fry muttered.

"What kind of moves you want this week?" George repeated.

"NONE," Fry repeated. "Just belt me around the head
and shoulders."

"Who in the hell have you got?"

"Stautner."

News of Tom's removing his ring traveled fast. Don
Meredith mentioned the fact in passing on the Monday-
night telecast of the Detroit game, and sportswriter Frank
Luksa carried a column on the incident. His source was an
anonymous player. The article did not go over well. Tom
lectured, "There are signs posted throughout NFL locker
rooms that say, *What You See Here, What You Hear Here,
What You Say Here, Stays Here.* This applies to us too.
Any player who doesn't have the guts to use his name in
an article like that has lost all my respect and doesn't deserve to be on this team."

I recall something similar that happened two years ago.
We had a team meeting, coaches excluded, to discuss the
Rentzel affair. The next day the gist of the entire meeting
was in the morning paper for all to read. This points up the
fact that a team is never as cohesive as one is led to believe. Everyone has friends on the outside, and sometimes
a reporter with a sympathetic ear is the best friend a
player's got. At any rate, nothing stays secret for very long.

San Diego upcoming. Duane Thomas worked out with
the Chargers for the first time this Friday, and rumor has it
that he has signed a contract and will be ready to suit up
for the game. If we should lose the game, and Duane is
any factor at all, it would not surprise me if Thomas quit

his team again. Duane steadfastly maintains that the Cowboys rode to two Super Bowls on his shoulders. A good performance by him, coupled with a San Diego victory, would, in his mind, lend credibility to his theory.

A harbinger of the Duane Thomas spirit surfaced in Dallas, circa 1964, in the form of Peter Gent, a former college basketball player, turned pro receiver. Gent was blessed with mediocre physical abilities; he was a gangling lad, slow afoot, with fair hands but a keen mind. Although Thomas and Gent were dissimilar in talents and personalities, they moved through similar intellectual planes, and ultimately arrived at the same assessment of Coach Landry: to them he was a non-person. Thomas labeled Coach Landry a plastic man. Gent sensed a paradox. In a recent interview for *Texas Monthly* magazine, Gent expounded on Thomas' characterization: "Landry *is* a plastic man. Yet, in Landry's presence, you do not feel the cool platitudes of plastic and computers . . . you feel something more visceral. You feel fear."

Gent's front line of defense was a lampoonist's sense of humor. On one Sunday in 1967 the Cowboys played the Colts in Baltimore. Gent entered the fray for only one play. Following the game, he bit into a chunk of hard candy and lost a front tooth. Early Monday morning, Pete showed up at the training room and convinced the trainers he had suffered the injury during the game (the club would then pay for the dental work). Tom, as was his custom then, came by to check on his injured charges.

"Walt, you all right? Anything serious, Lee Roy? . . . Pete? What in the world happened to you?"

Gent displayed a gap-toothed smile. "Well," he explained, "I got in for that one play, you know. . . . It was a near-o pinch and I had to block down on Bubba Smith. I hit him low and grabbed his leg . . . but he started to spin away . . . so I bit him as hard as I could on the Achilles tendon. I left my tooth in his calf."

Tom did an abrupt about-face and tromped out of the room.

"The more I'd fuck with Tom," Pete said, "the fairer he'd try to be with me." For many years this was Tom's approach to aberrant ballplayers: fairness above all. Duane was the first severe test for that policy, and after his coming, Tom found himself using two different standards in dealing with his players: one for Duane and one for the rest of the club. This proved to be a debilitating situation for Coach Landry and eventually he shipped Thomas off. What he did, however, was trade a bad dream for a nightmare. At the insistence of Sid Gillman, Bill Parks came over from San Diego in the Thomas trade. Physically, Parks was a premiere receiver, but his attitude was questionable. Could he function within a given system with a given set of rules and traditions? He could not.

As we took the field for our third game of the season (with Green Bay), Parks was to be our starting receiver. Billy reported to Coach Landry, on the sidelines, that he couldn't play—he just didn't feel like it. At another point in the year he again refused to play, this time because his close friend Tody Smith was ill with mononucleosis.

These developments marked the end of the Cowboy policy of accommodation. The screws have tightened now; the rules are spelled out, the the fines are stiff. There are no exceptions to anything.

"We have got to get ready for the Chargers tomorrow. San Diego is on the blink of being out of it, and it's our job to finish them off." Tom was getting us ready.

The San Diego affair was strange. Although we did prevail, we did not play well (again). We were ahead 31–0, with six minutes to play in the third quarter, when Hadl went berserk. The object of his madness was our novice cornerback, Charlie Waters. Coach Landry had completed the phase-out of Herb Adderley, and this was Charlie's first start. He was blown out. Hadl hit on four long bombs, three of them over Charlie; if the game had lasted another five minutes, we would have lost. Final score: 34–28, Dallas.

The highlight (?) of the afternoon was Duane. He had been activated just before the game and was in uniform for the first time that year. He came out to warm up, resplendent in his black high-tops, and was greeted with a chorus of boos. He shuffled into the far end zone and planted himself there, hands on knees, head down, for fifteen minutes. His teammates were scurrying around him in the pregame preparation, and Duane . . . just stood there. After a time (forever), he eased into his stance and jogged a short sprint. He turned around, jogged back, and reassumed his tuck position in the end zone. The crowd was delirious. For the remainder of the game, every Thomas movement was greeted with a cheer. He didn't play, but he did manage to wander around during the National Anthem. I wonder if footfall has a travesty rule.

After the offense had blown a couple of drives at the outset of the second half, Tom called them together and literally told them to get their collective heads out of their collective asses. He also said, "You can either get out there now and play some football, or get your asses chewed out on Tuesday." Interesting, for three reasons: (1) the use of the word "ass" (twice), (2) the fact that he expressed his feelings before the end of the game, and (3) the revelation that he is aware of the hatred of his film sessions.

Tom spoke Tuesday on mental image. He mentioned that some folks get up in the morning and are tired before they clamber out of bed. "These people have no mental image of themselves or what their day is about," Tom explained. He doesn't think we have the proper mental picture of ourselves and what we can accomplish. "Look at the Redskins," he said, gesturing. "They are in control of themselves as a unit. They see themselves as champions. We don't."

Another of our problems aside from a poorly developed mental picture and the presence of too many prima donnas and weak sisters, is rampant dissatisfaction. In college athletics I learned what I thought was a fundamental principle that could be applied to all sports: winning solves most of your problems, whether you are a player or a coach. I find this is not the case. Locker-room conversation is centered on leaving or retiring. Such talk is commonplace in training camp, of course—training camp is a bitch; but when you are 6–2 at midseason, ready for the stretch drive, dissatisfaction is incomprehensible. It is particularly disturbing when the unrest lies in the stars who are the backbone of the franchise. Among others, Mel Renfro, Bob Hayes, George Andrie, Chuck Howley, Lee Roy Jordan, and Bob Lilly have all expressed a strong desire to get out. There is something fundamentally wrong here.

Walt was telling this story on Charlie to the early crew yesterday morning: Charlie, in his debut at cornerback against San Diego, was burned two or three times for touchdowns, and he was deeply concerned. So concerned, Walt related, that he dropped into a local psychiatrist's office for an overhaul. After a grueling interview and hours of exhaustive research, the doctor announced his good news: "Charlie, you do not suffer from an inferiority complex."

"Aaaaaahhhhh," sighed Charlie.

"No," he said, "you're just physically inferior."

Charlie's real problem out at the corner is the fact that he has never played the position. His natural slot, in accordance with his size, speed, and Coach Landry's evaluation, is inside, at either strong or free safety. However, with the demise of Herb Adderley, we had a desperate need to fill that position, and Tom (ignoring the fact that white people haven't played the corner . . . well . . . since he did) felt Charlie could fill the bill. Tom may very well be right. Charlie started off on the wrong foot against

Hadl, but last week, against St. Louis, he intercepted two passes, returning one for a touchdown.

In the line, a player's mistakes are covered by the thunderous confusion of the pit; the corner, as the cliché goes, is the loneliest spot on the field. Charlie is in quick agreement. "It's a mindfucker," he said, ". . . all that space . . . all that green . . . it's like a long shot in pool. Since I'm so damned slow, my only chance is to hit the receiver hard before he gets into his route, then recover and try to stay with him for awhile."

Most teams employ cornerbacks who are compact packages of instinct and ability; their job is to line up on the receiver and run with him step-for-step. Dallas corners must play a more disciplined game.

"The first thing Tom wants you to do," Charlie explained, "is key the guards for run. If the guards pull you force. If they don't pull you check the quarterback for a quick set, . . . the off-back for flow, . . . only then do you find the receiver, and he could be running one of ninety-seven routes. It takes a machine to handle it all."

The worst possible situation is one in which the opposing team has the ball inside our twenty-yard line—the "freak zone," Charlie calls it. It's strictly a guessing game there; make the play and you've done your job, miss it and you're a goat. Charlie is getting all the action, regardless of field position; All-World Mel Renfro, who is on the opposite corner, has seen only six passes all season.

"I don't know how long I can take it," Charlie said, "before I flip out completely."

Charlie's shift to the corner has brought a welcome end to the deterioration in his relationship with Cliff. The constant bickering has been replaced with amiable conversation, and well it should be; they need each other now.

We opened our week's preparation for the Philadelphia Eagles with another meeting of the team (not including the coaching staff), led by our appointed co-captains, Bob

Lilly and Rayfield Wright. The message they intended to convey was terse and to the point: "We have arrived at the time of the season when we must get together as a team, ignore outside distractions, and play stretch football."

Rayfield was barely into his delivery when Calvin Hill stood up, eyes bulging, and stuttered through a meandering charge of racial injustice. "Take endorsements for example," Calvin said, cleverly not mentioning his three-year, $75,000 contract with Dr. Pepper. "Ron Sellers has been here six months and he has already done a Datsun commercial and is driving a complimentary 240Z. Mel Renfro has been here nine years and has never seen the day!"

"Waaaiiiiitt just a minute there." It was Sellers, and he was headed for the podium. Sellers proceeded to give a long spiel on his hardships with the New England Patriots, followed by a meticulous explanation of the Datsun deal—which needed no explanation. I have always been under the impression that companies spending money on an athlete's endorsement know precisely who they want and what they want to say. If the companies themselves don't know, then they hire ad agencies to tell them. It's no secret that football *stars,* black or white, get most of the commercials. I don't recall a football club voting on who would get this or that commercial.

Calvin's charges particularly infuriated the players of non-superstar status. He implied that the white boys were all over the TV screens making big bucks. I personally have done one commercial in five years, for a paltry two hundred dollars. I was in Utah following the '72 Super Bowl, and anxious to capitalize on the "Super Bowl bonanza" that you hear about. I hustled a single ad for the Utah Dodge dealers—"Meeting the challenge is the name of the game . . . in football . . . and in driving"—and quickly forgot about the endorsement end of the football business.

The meeting was getting out of hand when Mel finally spoke up. "The point Bob and Rayfield were trying to make at the beginning of this fiasco was that each individual must prepare himself for his job, and then execute correctly. If everyone does that, we can pull if off."

Bob took the cue and quickly closed down the meeting.

The length of the session tried Tom's patience. "I don't want to underestimate the importance of your meeting; I know it's important or you wouldn't have called it. However, I can't afford the time. If you want a team meeting, from now on it will have to be on your own time."

Squelch.

Larry ("Bubber") Cole has been idled since he tore some ligaments against Pittsburgh six weeks ago.

"How am I doing, Doc?" Larry inquired of Dr. Evans during the weekly probe.

Dr. Evans, who is gradually replacing retiring team physician Marvin Knight, was too involved in the examination to answer. Cole was stretched out on his back, with his leg extended into the air. Doc Evans had Larry by the ankle and was performing a subtle series of contortions with his leg to determine the flexibility and/or pain of the injured joint as it moved through a wide range of motions.

"Well, Larry," Dr. Evans said at length, "your leg is coming along fine. You ought to be ready to go in two or three weeks."

"By the San Francisco game?" Larry hedged.

"Certainly," said the doctor, "no problem."

"That's next week."

"Well, I don't think so."

Twenty-five minutes later Coach Landry activated Cole for this week's Philadelphia game, much to the shock of both Cole and Dr. Evans.

Thursday, November 16. Tom apologized for his shortness of temper yesterday when the meeting ran longer than it should have. "I thought you were talking about the Players Association in there," Tom said. "Anytime you're talking football, take all the time you want."

Walt Garrison, despite one of his traumatic rituals of pain, played a superb game in our 28–7 victory over Philly. Admittedly, Walt plays injured more than anyone would care too, but the remarkable thing about these performances is that they vary only slightly from his normal, healthy, outstanding games. When I was a rookie we were to play San Francisco in Kezar Stadium for the 1970 NFC championship. I hadn't seen Garrison all week prior to the game, so I assumed that the beating he had taken in the opening round of the play-offs had sidelined him indefinitely. When the offense took the field that Sunday, however, Walt was ready. Going into the game, Walt was suffering muscle spasms in his back and a sprained ligament in his knee; by the end of the game he had sustained a sprained right ankle and a fractured right clavicle. He had to be carried into the locker room when it was all over. Despite the injuries, he somehow managed to gain fifty-two yards and catch some crucial passes.

People often wonder how Walt is physically able to take the abuse inevitably inflicted on a smallish running back over the years. I am amazed he is even still alive. Several days prior to the '72 Pro Bowl, Walt took a gash to the head in some bulldogging event and almost had to miss the game. Almost. Consider the most recent (Philadelphia) incident. Walt is a whittler from way back. He is very serious about his craft, and the tools of his craft. He had acquired a new knife earlier in the week and spent the better part of three days honing, stropping, whetting, grinding, and doing all those things you do to a knife to get a fine, sharp edge that will shave the hair clean off your arm. Saturday night was the night, and Walt took a three-finger dip of Skoal and settled back to some serious, new-knife whittling. He was piling up shavings at an alarming rate when the blade slipped and nearly cleaved off his left index finger. It was hanging by a thin hunk of flesh. Blood was everywhere.

"It might take a few stitches," Walt thought out loud, but the trainers and Doc Knight were out on the town, trying to make the best of Philadelphia. It had to wait. Sunday morning, Dr. Knight put eighteen sutures into the finger, wrapped a Band-Aid around it, and sent him on his way. Walt didn't even fumble.

Verne Lundquist, local sports director for an ABC affiliate, visited the practice field and came away with a classic Dave Manders interview:

VERNE: Tell us, Dave, how were you tagged with the nickname "Dog"?

MANDERS: I don't know, Verne; you'll have to ask my wife.

For our third outing in eleven days, we played the San Francisco 49ers on Thanksgiving Day in Texas Stadium. Unfortunately, we were looking forward more to the weekend than to the 49ers, and they throttled us 30–10.

The events of the first half pretty much indicated that a victory was not in the cards on this day. On our second possession in the game we drove to their six and fumbled. The next drive resulted in a Dallas score, and we were threatening again late in the second quarter when Craig faded to pass and lost the ball to an onrushing lineman. The guy headed due north with the football and scored. At the half we were down 14–10 instead of ahead 21–7. The game degenerated from there.

My individual battle with Len Rohde, a salty, thirteen-year veteran, began inauspiciously and quickly swung in his favor. I was sporting a heavy cast on my right hand to protect a broken bone incurred against St. Louis several weeks before. On one particular, typical play, Brodie faded to pass, Rohde dropped back to protect, and I took off for the quarterback. Rohde grabbed me, one hand under each armpit, and successfully pinched my pectoral muscles against the breastplate of my shoulder pads (an unethical ploy if there ever was one). I yelled—and belted Rohde full in the head with my seven pounds of plaster. The cast shattered on impact, my hand began to throb, and Rohde didn't even acknowledge the lick, he just turned and trotted back to the huddle.

The club now stands 8–3, with three games remaining. We must win all three to clinch a spot for the play-offs.

After a debacle of the magnitude just experienced, Tom's reactions are stereotyped. You can usually count on a good old-fashioned ass-chewing at the minimum, or, at the maximum, on an ass-chewing combined with a sperm count. Tom's sperm counts are not literal, of course, but the Zero Club has conceived of a Sperm Count Program which would enable a head coach to weed out his lesser men as early in the season as training camp. The head coach could then forgo the insulting assaults on his team's virility, pride, etc., and spend his time more profitably, watching film. Unfortunately, few coaches have shown an interest in subscribing to the revolutionary program, so speeches like the one Tom was about to deliver are still in vogue around the league.

Tom began modestly by criticizing the offense for not being tough and the defense for not moving. Then, mentioning an article by Bob St. John in the Dallas *Morning News*, Tom became angry. St. John had casually stated that the current edition of the Dallas Cowboys reminded him of the wishy-washy '68–'69 club.

"That hurts me," Tom said. "That hurts me. We're po-

tentially so much better than that '68–'69 team that it isn't
even funny. Yet we go out and play a game like we did
Thursday. It's pitiful. I'll tell you, . . . I'm just not built
like that. I got too much pride to sit back and be humili-
ated like that. When you get beat like we did, there's only
one thing I know to do and that's work harder. Heckfire!
We're right in the middle of a championship drive and
we're playing like the Houston Oilers! You've got to work
and you've got to fight for what you get. We're not doing
anything—I guarantee you that's going to change. Anybody in here who is not prepared to fight and work with
everything he's got for three more weeks can get up and
leave right now. I'll be more than happy to put your name
on the reserve list for the rest of the year. I don't need you.

"Look," Tom said, calming down. "One of the big difficulties in life is to become a man. I've seen thirty-five-
year-old men who are still children. Some of us make it,
some of us don't. It's going to take men to make the push
for the championship."

Yesterday, Don Cochren went into the coach's dressing
room to put up the daily injury reports. Coach Stallings
was in the room at the time and observed the flaking wall-
board and numerous holes that have resulted from years of
tacking up injury reports.

"You know, Don," Gene drawled, "I'm not trying to tell
you your business, but wouldn't it be easier if you just
put up an old bulletin board instead of punishing yourself and that wall so much?"

"That's not a bad idea, Gene," Don replied as he turned
to go; "I'll do it."

"Aw hell, Cocky, forget it," Gene said. "I don't want you
to be the first son-of-a-bitch around here to take my advice."

One of the flight approaches into the St. Louis airport
runs parallel with the Mississippi River and affords a nice

view of the Gateway Arch in downtown St. Louis. When D. D. Lewis was a rookie and making the St. Louis trip for the first time, he noticed the unusual monument and was puzzled. "Say, Ralph, is St. Louis the national head-quarters for McDonald's?"

For some vague reason I am finding it difficult to pre-pare myself mentally to play the Cardinals . . . again . . . especially in St. Louis. We never seem to play the Cards in a meaningful football game. Our games are always ei-ther early in the season, when the division races are in chaos, or late in the season, when games with noncon-tenders become mere formalities.

Aside from the short flight home, the only thing I enjoy about St. Louis is Harold's Tattoo Parlor and Rifle Range. Harold's is not quaintly tucked away, as one might expect; it is convenient to our hotel and mighty handy if you enjoy collecting .22 short shell cases and snorting cheap gun-powder. It's the sort of place one should share with one's friends. Blaine and I decided that Saturday night we would get farmer Cole drunk and smuggle him over to Harold's to secure for him a suitable etching; we settled on a plow, circumscribed by Cole's motto: "Born to Raise Wheat."

Cole overheard our plans. When we got to St. Louis, he locked himself in the bathroom.

The Cardinal game was festooned with penalties, and we were the primary beneficiaries. At one point Mike Ditka leaped off the bench in disgust, grabbed one of the officials, and spun him around.

"Say," he said, "are you a member of the Fellowship of Christian Athletes?" Mike was surprisingly calm.

"No," the official answered.

"WELL, FUCK YOU!!" Mike screamed.

The yellow flag flew again.

We defeated the unmotivated Cardinals 27–6 and moved immediately into intensive preparation for the Redskin game; we must beat Washington to clinch a play-off berth.

Our film study of the Washington offense yielded some interesting points. On first glance, their offensive personnel, to a man, seemed to be sluggish, not moving with authority. A-ha, we said. On closer examination, however, the defensive team was seen to be moving in the same unhurried manner. It turned out that the Washington photographer shoots his film at a faster frame speed than normal, hence the slow-motion effect. He must be getting paid according to film footage.

A pertinent point we also noted was the unusual alignment of their offensive line. The linemen are almost three feet off the line of scrimmage. I'm sure there must be some timing advantages associated with the running backs, and the extra distance gives the line more momentum as they move into their blocking assignments, but it also gives the defensive player more time to take his keys. The real advantages are unclear. Bob further observed that right guard John Wilbur, a former Cowboy, does not always stay the required yard off the ball. In fact, on a running play, or a play-action pass, Wilbur cheats up twelve inches. Similarly, when he has to pull, Wilbur slides back perceptibly and thus tips the play. Wilbur is a hustler, but the scouting report questions his ability, and he may be compensating in these small ways for a lack of technique. The other point we detected was that Kilmer moves his foot a split second before he receives the snap from Hauss. Now, if we could somehow watch his foot during the game. . . .

We won the game 34–24 without the benefit of observing Kilmer's foot action. We took a 28–3 lead into the dressing room at half time, and then held on for the victory. In terms of injuries, it was a costly triumph. Charley Taylor cracked back on Chuck Howley in the second half and destroyed Chuck's knee. Taylor came in low, unusual for him, and rolled into Hoggy's firmly planted leg. Chuck is out for the season and will probably be forced into an early retirement.

The defensive secondary, acutely aware of Taylor to begin with, pounded him unmercifully. Late in the game he dropped one perfectly thrown pass, and coughed up another for an interception and a touchdown; he was hit simultaneously by three people.

Billy Zeoli was in for the Sunday-morning devotional before the Redskin game, and for a change, we won a game he attended. Billy admitted at the outset of the meeting that he had run out of material, so he brought along a thirty-minute film clip of Gospel Film's latest effort, "The Life of Dave Boyer." Dave Boyer, you'll recall, was the reformed night-club singer who performed for us in training camp several years ago, singing gospel hits. At the end of this morning's session, Billy promised to forward a copy of the sound-track album as soon as it was available.

Sufficiently bolstered, I proceeded to the stadium to harness up for the Skins. It is incredible what dashes through the mind on the day of a big football game.

Our fans were moderately interested in this, the key game of the season. They generally tend to sit on their hands until something spectacular happens. The ladies playing bridge in the fifty-thousand-dollar boxes may get excited over an eighty-five-yard scoring play. What I'm trying to say is that there is a noted lack of spontaneity at Cowboy games. The club management is more than aware of the nonchalance of Texas Stadium fans, and since this was a *National Telecast*, unprecedented procedures were required to stimulate our people to the appropriate level of enthusiasm.

When the tempo of the game dictated some fan encouragement, the stadium PA announcer was instructed to hit the airwaves: "GO . . . GO . . . GO. . . ." The fans took up the charge from the fourth "GO," and faded by the sixth. This is the first time such an innovative departure has been utilized, and incidentally, it is against league rules (as are club-donated gratuities—Christmas gifts, turkeys at Thanksgiving, all "detrimental to football," somebody has decreed). Up in the press box the crowd is not audible, but the PA is courteously piped in as a reminder that there is a game underway. It was quite humorous when the normally sophisticated announcer took to leading cheers.

A mild controversy has arisen from the ashes of the Washington game. George Allen has accused Coach Landry of devising an illegal block specifically designed to maim Redskin linebackers. Jack Pardee has labeled the block "vicious and illegal, taught by a coach with a 'holier than thou' attitude."

Alworth was flanked right and Pardee was the backer on that side. On a sign from Morton, Lance started in motion back toward the quarterback. The ball was snapped and Alworth went after Pardee, cutting him down. Apparently Pardee sprained his knee and had to leave the game. Ironically, the slow-motion replays showed Alworth hitting Pardee with a perfectly legal crack-back block. On the other hand, Charley Taylor's lick on Howley was extremely questionable and could easily have been called a clip.

Meanwhile, George Allen, whose proud defense yielded thirty-four points and 267 yards on the ground, has set up an effective smoke screen. George has convinced the Washington press that an injustice was committed and they have been interrogating Coach Landry on the Alworth crack-back! When we watched the films of the game and saw the play in question, everyone wondered what in the hell Pardee was bellyaching about. Mike Ditka exploded out of his chair and screamed at the screen, "Pardee!! You chickenshit pussy!!" Even Tom cracked a smile on that one.

The NFL Players Association monthly newsletter carried this interesting highlight in the December issue: "Coach J. D. Roberts of the New Orleans Saints has announced a $10,000 fine for any player talking to newspapers about the team."

We have now clinched a wild-card berth in the play-offs, and will tentatively play the 49ers in the opening round. Lost in the furor over the Washington game and the excitement generated by the Cowboys' seventh consecutive appearance in the play-offs, is the fact that we must still play the New York Giants in the regular-season finale.

The anticlimactic Giant game was a nightmare; they ate us up 23–3. We were not in the proper frame of mind to play a football game. Prior to the contest the usual bull session among the early arrivals turned into a heated bitch. All the stories told had one element in common: gouging by the Cowboy management. Lee Roy Jordan spoke of cold negotiating techniques and perennial low pay. Dan Reeves described his abrupt phase-out from coach to inactive player. Bob Lilly had enlisted management aid in a highly emotional divorce proceeding and they apparently reneged at the last minute. By the time Tom and the rest of the staff arrived at the stadium, Mel Renfro, Dave Manders, and Jethro Pugh had added their comments. The atmosphere was anything but positive, and it showed in the game.

Alex Hawkins, the controversial color man for the telecast of the game, was bewildered. "I realize the Cowboys have the play-offs clinched," he said, "but they are really playing poorly. I don't know. This is a puzzling team in more ways than one. Right now you've got Calvin Hill in the dressing room with an upset stomach . . . and Walt Garrison out there playing with cracked ribs. I just can't figure it."

Friday, December 22. We landed at San Francisco International Airport and immediately boarded the chartered buses. We were bound for some motel on El Camino Real, and then a short afternoon workout at Candlestick Park. As everyone settled on the bus, two short, fat women bolted past the driver and approached Roger Staubach midway down the aisle. They were giggling incessantly.

"Are you Roger Staubach?"

"Yes."

"Will you sign this?" they asked, presenting Roger with a team photograph of the Fremont Frogs, 1972 Junior League champions.

Roger obliged, as is his custom, and no sooner had he lifted pen from picture than the ladies' true purpose crystallized. "YEA, 49ERS!!!" they screamed, and waddled off the bus as fast as they had got on. Toni Fritsch stood up in the back of the bus, cleared his throat, and said in his most gutteral English: "Only in Amerikka . . ."

The San Francisco game could have been part of a movie. It was the most incredible game I have ever witnessed or participated in.

Vic Washington began the proceedings on an ominous note when he returned the opening kick ninety-seven yards for a quick touchdown. We were sour, and we stayed sour until the final six minutes of the fourth quarter. With 6:02 left, Fritsch kicked a twenty-seven-yard field goal, making the score 28–16. There didn't seem to be enough time. Staubach, who hadn't played a game since August, was directing the attack. The defense held, and with 1:20 remaining, Staubach hit Billy Parks for a twenty-yard touchdown. Toni Fritsch then magically reverse-footed an onside kick and Mel Renfro completed the unbelievable play by recovering the football at midfield. Three plays later, Ron Sellers caught the clinching touchdown. Final score: 30–28.

Dave Wilcox, the outstanding 49er linebacker, had to

have oral surgery immediately following the game; his foot had become lodged in his mouth. The previous week on KRLD's "Countdown to Kick-off" show, Al Wisk had asked Wilcox what he wanted for Christmas. Wilcox said that he had heard Walt Garrison had purchased a ranch with his Super Bowl money. "But," he said, "this year I'm buying the ranch, and after the season I'd like to invite Walt up for a little visit."

With two minutes left in the game, Wilcox was bellowing at our offense across the line of scrimmage: "Now, you sons-of-bitches, you're going to find out what it's like to lose to us!!! HAAA!" When Sellers scored the winning touchdown, Wilcox hurled his helmet a record forty feet into the air. Too bad.

As we slogged into the locker room at half time, down 21–13, Billy Zeoli was guarding the tunnel entrance. When he saw us he held up a hand-lettered sign on an old piece of cardboard. It said, "NEVER GIVE UP."

With the National Conference title game approaching, there is some question as to whom Tom will go with at quarterback. Staubach's heroics against the 49ers have vaulted him into contention with Morton. Craig may very well find himself on the bench for the crucial game of the season.

Many of the offensive players feel that Roger, although incredible last week, was explicably rusty, and even at his best, does not possess Craig's capacity to read defenses. The case for Craig is predicated on this ability to read defenses and on the fact that he led us to a 10–4 season and a play-off slot. Furthermore, Morton has proven to be particularly effective against the Redskins; in two regular-season games this year the offense put up fifty-four points—no small task against a fine Washington defense.

Saturday afternoon I found a letter in my box at the Marriott from Billy Zeoli. "This is a photostatic copy of the sign I held up last week at half time. . . ." And sure enough, there it was again: "NEVER GIVE UP."

Tom elected to go with Roger, the rationale probably being his performance in the Super Bowl drive last year coupled with the magic of the 49er game. The Morton faction was disgusted, especially after the Skins devoured us 26–3. The Washington defensive end, Ron McDole, noted that Roger could not locate his secondary receiver; he held the ball too long and was subsequently trapped a number of times. Diron Talbert figured it was an injustice to throw Roger into a championship game: "Hell, he hasn't worked all season. We felt it was to our advantage for him to play."

Jack Pardee inquired after Tex Schramm. "I'd like to ask Tex about his dynasty," Pardee said. "That's all we've been hearing about since last year's Super Bowl. . . . If a dynasty is what they had, you might call us dynasty-breakers."

I asked a local sportswriter if he thought Craig would be back, in view of his abrupt banishment. "In six years they'll have retirement ceremonies for Morton out at Texas Stadium," he said. "Coach Landry will present him with his other testicle."

Midway through the third period, Charlie Waters fielded a Redskin punt and attempted a return; he took two steps and was buried by the Washington coverage. Charlie didn't get up. He lay writhing in the dirt, clutching his left arm . . . begging for a sedative; the bone connecting his shoulder and elbow was broken in half. The doctors set his arm on the field and helped him to the locker room.

Post-game. Charlie, one arm in a splint, the other wrapped around Cliff for support, staggered from the locker room and eased onto the players' bus. The Demerol had taken its numbing effect; the pain was now sporadic. An ambulance was alerted to meet our chartered flight in Dallas.

As the 707 started its descent into Dallas, Charlie Waters, staring bleary-eyed on the Metroplex, concisely summed up the year. "Well," he murmured, "I just hope the off-season lasts as long as the season did. . . ."

It never does.

4

RETAINING
A PEDESTAL

The off-season, going away, lasted only a tenth of a second.

On July 16, 1973, the Dallas-based Cowboy players assembled at Love Field for the first leg of the annual trek to Thousand Oaks and another training camp. Bob Lilly ambled onto the American Airlines flight and slumped heavily into an aisle seat in the first-class section. Bob glanced uncomfortably around the cabin and sensed a flaw; some familiar faces were missing. The younger guys were there—Waters, Garrison, Cole—but notably absent were Bob's contemporaries, his two close friends George Andrie and Chuck Howley. George and Chuck had been Bob's running mates for over a decade of Dallas Cowboy football, and now they had retired. Lilly was alone as the old man of the team. The fabric of the club was clearly changing, and Bob, once a hub of the Cowboy team, was being metamorphosed into another spoke. Time was the sad culprit.

Bob noticed Larry Cole sitting in front of him, and leaned forward and tapped Cole on the shoulder.

"I'll tell you one thing," Bob said, "this is going to be a big year for me. I've eased up on the weights this year so my back feels better and . . ."

Cole was emotionally involved with a copy of *Fortune* magazine, so he wasn't paying much attention. Larry noted that his newly formed construction company (Larry Cole Builders, Inc.) would have to increase sales by a multiple of fifty million if it were ever to make the "Fortune 500."

"Fine, Bob," Larry mumbled, and dozed off.

Lilly ordered cocktails. He and George Andrie customarily arrived in Thousand Oaks well lubricated, and Bob was determined to uphold that tradition. The saga of Bob and George reached a high point last year, when, after they had consumed gallons of vodka tonic, quinine showed up in their urine tests in the camp physical. Tex Schramm became concerned. Heroin, you see, is often cut with quinine, and the preposterous notion arose that Lilly and Andrie might have been experimenting with hard drugs. The doctors finally laid the matter to rest by explaining the chemical nature of vodka tonic and the effect it has on one's piss.

Lilly ordered more cocktails. Time passed, and Cole awoke to the harsh strains of a very different Bob Lilly. The optimism he had expressed at the outset of the flight had vanished; Lilly was now bitching a blue streak. The core of the bitch centered on the Cowboy management's insensitve dealings with some long-time veterans, and on a nugget of information he had uncovered at the Pro Bowl in January. It was this: Merlin Olsen (a comparable player with a comparable career) was making nearly twice the money Bob was.

"I'm through," Bob concluded as he and Larry rode the moving sidewalk to the American Airlines baggage claim. "Fuck 'em."

Lilly picked up his baggage, hopped an Air West shuttle to Las Vegas, dropped a quick $2,500, and flew home.

Training camp was in a shambles. Lilly had departed, Dave Manders had never left Dallas, and Craig Morton reported and then walked out. Lee Roy Jordan, Jethro Pugh, and Mel Renfro were in camp, but barely. All three were unsigned and seriously close to walking out themselves. The bitterness that had simmered untended through the '72–'73 season had finally surfaced; the basic stability of the club was threatened.

Club president Tex Schramm privately visualized the upheaval as a vindictive player conspiracy aimed at discrediting his organization and gaining public sympathy in ongoing contract negotiations. The "conspirators" were Lee Roy Jordan, Dave Manders and Bob Lilly; the public outlet for the "conspiracy" was Frank Luksa's column in the Dallas *Times Herald*. Tex's theory of collusion, however, proved to be feeble, though convenient.

Luksa had stumbled on the story in May when he dropped by the practice field and observed the Off-Season Workout Program Tote Board. The Off-Season Workout Program Tote Board is a chart, placed prominently in the locker room, listing all players who live in Dallas and how many times they have worked out during the three-month, supervised program (the program is voluntarily mandatory). Luksa noted that Jordan, Lilly, and Manders had not worked out at all, so he contacted the trio to determine the reasons for their lack of participation. The problem revolved around the two points of player–management interaction: contracts and compensation.

Through the years, many of the longtime Dallas veterans had trusted Tex Schramm for a determination of their fair market value. "Pay me what I'm worth," they always said, and Tex never did. This is how a Robert Lilly could play twelve brilliant years for the Dallas Cowboys only to discover he had been viciously underpaid all along (joining Lilly in that department would be Manders, Jordan, Pugh, Renfro, Howley, Andrie, ad infinitum).

So, basic compensation was a problem. Also at issue was management's sluggish approach to contract negotiations. Customarily, a player up for a new contract would find himself unsigned as training camp opened. Whether discussion had been initiated in January or June, serious negotiating never took place until the opening of camp. Why? Because then the player was at a distinct disadvantage. Training camp is a bitch; you are mentally and physically exhausted, and it can be quite irritating to spend rest and recuperation time haggling over a contract with Gil Brandt or Tex Schramm. The major point is that you are forced to play football every day without a contract. This impairs your concentration, and a semiserious injury destroys any bargaining position you may have had.

Lee Roy, Dave, and Bob explained all this to Luksa and emphasized that it would be best for the team if training camp opened clear of any contract hassles; concentration would then be focused on the task at hand.

"Do you want to go public with this?" Luksa asked.

"No," was the unanimous response. The Cowboys disdain negotiating through the press; the players wanted to give the club every opportunity to reach a settlement before the story reached the newspapers.

Luksa sat on the story for a month and then checked back with Jordan. No effort had been made. The story broke.

The rest of the team completely approved of the revelations made in the ensuing articles; any player who had been around awhile had suffered through the same kind of disconcerting treatment. The younger players were especially concerned; if management mistreated the backbone of the franchise, then what could they expect in the way of future consideration? The situation was serious.

Texas E. Schramm did nothing to check the downward spiral of team morale. Instead, he placed his faith in the homing instincts of his veteran players; he trusted their emotional and economic reliance on the game to outweigh any superficial crust of individual pride. Tex was perfectly willing to let Manders retire and Jordan play out his option, if, indeed, they really would; Lilly, however, had thrown him a knuckle ball.

Bob had come to terms just prior to the opening of camp, but lingering bitterness over his contractual situation, and

perhaps some empathy with his teammates, had prompted
his failure to report. When Tex learned of Lilly's west-
coast turnaround, he blew out of camp like a rookie on
waivers. A press conference had been hastily called in
Dallas, ostensibly for Bob to announce his retirement, but
Tex arrived at the eleventh hour and persuaded him to
come back.

Shortly thereafter, Craig Morton, ensconced in the pala-
tial Howard Johnson's at Thousand Oaks, reached a verbal
agreement with the club, and wandered back up the road
to training camp.

Dave Manders was allowed to retire. But as the exhibition season unfolded, footballs began to sail consistently
over punter Marv Bateman's head, and Manders, master of
the long snap, was retrieved.

Lee Roy Jordan played quietly through the preseason
without a contract. Despite the early hullabaloo and pro-
Jordan press, the Cowboys were apparently convinced that
this was to be Lee Roy's final season. If they could get Jordan for one more year at reduced rates (the option-year salary is 10 percent less than the previous year's salary), then
so much the better. The week before the first league game,
Lee Roy visited Tex in the Cowboy offices to discuss the
situation. The situation was this: either the Cowboys
would present Lee Roy with a decent contract, or Lee Roy
would retire. Lee Roy had thrown them a fork ball. Tom
Stincic had been the heir apparent to the middle-
linebacker position until he walked out of camp a year ago.
Rookie Rodrigo Barnes had assumed Stincic's role, but
Barnes was not yet experienced enough to take over.

Lee Roy got his contract.

Coach Landry responded to the situation by behaving
with uncharacteristic candor. When a decision was made,
trivial or significant, Tom brought it to the attention of the
team and elaborated on the reasons behind it. This is not
to say that the players or the assistant coaches shared in

the decision-making process—that power has never been shared. However, Coach Landry's openness vastly improved the quality of information available to the players, and we no longer had to rely so heavily on the grapevine.

The most meaningful part of Coach Landry's effort was an attempt at a more personal approach to his players. On the football field he became more active in his coaching. In the past he had played a passive role in practice, leaving most of the coaching to the assistants; now he moved briskly from drill to drill, pointing out fine points of technique or explaining the objectives of a particular defense, his focus always on the individual. Off the field, Tom was a veritable fountain of conversation; he said hello to anyone, inquired after families, and even cracked an occasional joke. It was evident that Tom was acting out of character, but it didn't matter; his enthusiasm was infectious, and he pulled the club together.

Tex Schramm attempted to follow Coach Landry's example, but only succeeded in smudging Tom's efforts. He met with the players one evening, purportedly to field questions concerning the current state of our embattled training camp, and how it got to be that way, but the results of the meeting were disappointing. Tex furnished only his name, rank, and serial number, and then closed the session with this gem: "I love you guys," he said, "that's the right word, isn't it? Love? Hell! You're my product!"

Ballplayers always suspect that they are nicely packaged chunks of product; nevertheless, it is deflating to be labeled as such by your boss. "Product," I always thought, applied to bars of soap. Fortunately, Tex retreated from the rush to sincerity and did not make himself available to the group for the rest of the season.

Training camp this year was tougher than it had ever been—more hitting, more running, longer hours—but a mutual good-feeling (uncharacteristic of training camp) came out of it, due in large part to Coach Landry himself. The esprit was typified by a "we can do anything" attitude, which in its off-field manifestations yielded some interesting results.

Cliff and I had retired late one night when Gene Stallings appeared on the hall. "Everybody in?!" he hollered, and began a cursory room check. There was some muffled scrambling in the room next to ours—unusual, since that room was supposed to be unoccupied.

"Cliff," I whispered, "take a look at this."

Our bathroom door was cracked, offering a limited view of the adjoining room. An assortment of black bodies, glistening with sweat, white teeth flashing, were gently hoisting the butt end of a large, pale female out the window. There was a thud.

"Oh, Lord," Cliff said.

The black bodies, chore completed, scampered for their rooms. I opened our window. The naked fat girl was wallowing exhausted in the flowerbed; her clothes were scattered everywhere. She was a summer-school coed.

"Can I help you?" I asked politely.

That scared her. She gathered up her clothes and ran yelping into the night.

We tested our collective mettle for the first time in an early exhibition game with a fine Oakland Raider team. It was a sinister evening; a thick fog boiled quickly in off the bay, shrouding the field and mixing nicely with Oakland's black home jerseys. We were led out for introductions by Lee Roy Jordan (small) and D. D. Lewis (also small). Oakland lumbered out under the auspices of Gene Upshaw (large) and Art Shell (extra large). Shell, 300 pounds of hongry and All-Pro, was my tackle for the game.

Oakland broke the huddle for the first play, and Shell, in keeping with the spirit of the evening, was wearing black leather gloves.

"Heh," I chuckled nervously. "Say, Art, . . . uh . . . what's with the gloves?"

"Nothin' man," he said. "I just don't want to mess up my knuckles—on your head."

The ball snapped, and Shell pummeled me.

Just prior to the half, Ernie Stautner called on one Harvey Othel Banks Martin, an immense, first-year defensive end, to enter the fray and do battle with Shell.

"What's he doin' to you?" Harvey asked before he went in.

"Stay away from him," I said. "He wants to hit and then hold; you can beat him around the corner." I forgot to tell him about the black gloves.

"Got it," he said.

Harvey set up on Shell's outside shoulder, poised and quivering in his stance. On the snap of the ball, Harvey detonated directly into Shell: they met head on. As Shell slammed his fists hard into Harvey's rib cage, his helmet ripped up and through Harvey's face. Poor Harv was instantaneously airborne, then on his butt—face guard smashed, blood trickling from his nose. Harvey weaved to the sidelines.

"I see what you mean," he said.

We eventually lost to Oakland, but no matter; the bright spots overshadow the defeat. Cliff Harris played well and should this year reach his ultimate dream, being an All-Pro. The offensive line is set with Wright, Nye, Fitzgerald, Niland, and Neely, and should be excellent. Morton and Staubach are firing, Drew Pearson and Otto Stowe are catching, and Calvin Hill and Walt Garrison are running with authority. During the off-season there was some question whether Charlie Waters would ever play football again. The broken arm he incurred against Washington last year failed to heal. He spent seven weeks in the hospital, finally emerging with a fourteen-inch steel rod embedded in his arm, and healthy dependence on Demerol. It took him three weeks to shuck the medication, and the rest of the time to rebuild his body strength. Charlie somehow managed, and he, too, played well against Oakland.

This edition of the Cowboys is markedly different, from the degree of player dedication to the attitude of the coaching staff. For the first time in years people are working together toward a common goal. Meetings are purposeful, practices are spirited, and at last I am enjoying myself.

The club responded heartily to Coach Landry's revamped approach and it was evident in our play. We were a solid 10–4 for the season, we won out over Washington for the Eastern Division title, and we advanced to the play-offs for the eighth consecutive year—an unprecedented feat in the annals of the NFL. Our loss to Minnesota in the 1973 NFC championship game took some of the luster off of our season, but the loss notwithstanding, it was a good year.

Coach Landry assembled the squad after the game and told us that this season had been one of his best, in fact, the most enjoyable he had experienced in a long time. The players shared his feelings.

July, 1974. I sit sweating and sweltering in my underwear; it is ground-cracking hot, there has been no rain in three months, and the goddamn air conditioner has given up. Texas-sized insects bang at the windows in another glorious southwestern summer.

My biological clock, calibrated through twelve years of the American football exeprience, tells me I should be uncomfortable: aching, sweating, itching, stinking, thirsting. . . . It tells me I should be in Thousand Oaks, California, away from my pregnant wife, tucked into a stucco dormitory with forty other men-boys in a state of suspended adolescence. 'It tells me I should be preparing for another season. Instead, I am at home. The NFL player-management collective-bargaining agreement hammered

out during the 1970 players' strike has expired; there has
been no progress in new negotiations, and another strike
has been called.

    As a rookie in 1970, awestruck with opportunity and
inundated by the complexities of modern professional-
football, I required time—time to adjust from the
free-wheeling atmosphere of a poor college-football program to the serious, strictly business aspects of professional football; time to assimilate the infinite refinements
in technique required by that transition. The 1970 players'
strike afforded me the time. I showed well in the early
phases of training camp while Willie Townes, my competition for a position then, was hampered by his absence. In
the end he was shipped off to New York, and I made the
team. There were eleven of us who did: myself, John
Fitzgerald, Charlie Waters, Cliff Harris, Duane Thomas,
Steve Kiner, Bob Asher, Doug Mooers, Margene Adkins,
Mark Washington, and Joe Williams. That was four years
ago.
    I am probably a bit more apprehensive sitting out the
present strike than Willie Townes was in 1970. After all,
there were no defensive linemen in camp then, just a
sixth-rounder who was picked on a dare, and a few oddball
free agents. All Townes had to do when he got to training
camp was play, which he didn't.
    My apprehension has nothing to do with performance; I
have been a front-line player for several years, and my
play has been creditable if not exceptional (my father
would take issue with that, of course). I have been in-
tegrated into the Landry defensive machine, and I appre-
ciate its finely tuned coordination and its aesthetic execu-
tion. My problem concerns ability. There is a player in
training camp this year who is being hailed as the hum-
minest son-of-a-bitch to hit the gridiron since Hash Marks.
His name is Ed Jones. He was the first player selected in
the last NFL draft. He is 6 feet 9 inches tall, weighs 265

pounds, and runs forty yards in 4.754 seconds. Unreal. Besides all those physical tools, Ed is blessed with that one necessary intangible to lead his assault on superstardom—a terrific nickname. Too Tall Jones can not miss.

He is warming up at my position.

So, I am faced this year with the same failure potential I encountered as a rookie. All the trappings are there. The prestige of the club is at stake, and nobody stands in the way of club prestige. The Cowboys selected Jones as the best, they touted him as the ultimate football lineman, and now he must play—not just play . . . *star*. Confronted with a better mousetrap, I can only hope for some undetected deficiency; perhaps Ed is not suited to Cowboy-style defense. . . . I don't know. It would serve no purpose to post an appearance in training camp; the coaching staff is already aware of my capabilities and limitations, going in would only heighten my anxiety. Besides, there is a strike in progress, and a smattering of principle lies buried in the ballyhoo.

The basic issues which led to the strike were muddled from the outset. The union leadership cried, "No Freedom, No Football," and adopted a clenched-first logo; the owners screamed social revolution and stamped the union leaders "radical"; newspapers around the country received a list of ninety player demands (with no accompanying rationale), and most of the sportswriters immediately fell in line with the owners. Consequently, the strike was pitched to the public on an emotional, irrational plane, and the gut issues were irretrievably lost.

Blaine Nye followed the nonprogress of the strike from his home in Menlo Park, California, where he was finishing his M.B.A. at Stanford. His input was the San Francisco *Chronicle*, and he noted with irritation the absence of a dispassionate, journalistic approach to the strike and its issues. The *Chronicle* ran a number of articles on the subject in which the players were portrayed as insufferable, pampered moneygrubbers. By the third week of this coverage, Blaine was thoroughly incensed; he vented his hostility at the typewriter, and the result was a clear, logical analysis of the decision to strike:

The dispute between the NFL players and owners seems quite complicated, with most people, including the participants themselves to some extent, failing to comprehend what the actual problems are. I think an excellent way of illustrating the situation is to use the analogy of an auction.

In an auction, if an item comes up for bid and all the bidders except one drop out early, the remaining bidder gets the item at a relatively low price, while, if at the same stage in the bidding there are two bidders left, they will bid each other up to a higher price. (This winning bid will continue to rise with the number of bidders but more slowly with increasing numbers, asymptotically approaching an upper limit.) Neither bidder will bid more than an item is worth to him, but nevertheless the item will sell for a higher price.

This fact of life has long been recognized by NFL owners and has led to the existing mechanisms for avoiding competitive bidding situations for football players. The result has been substantial owner savings in player salaries.

Clearly, these mechanisms violate players' Constitutional rights to choose their employer and to sell their services to the highest bidder. The owners have not in the smallest way similarly compromised their freedoms to make as much money as possible, to choose the players they want to play for them, to dictate contract wording or game rules, etc. This inequity is, to my way of thinking, the basis for the current strike.

The owners argue that no other system will

work and refuse to talk further on the subject. The obvious flaws in their arguments are (1) it is quite illegal to unilaterally deprive a player of his Constitutional rights, and (2) since no other system has ever been tried, it can only be assumed that the owners' desperate preoccupation with the existing system is deeply rooted in its advantages to them alone.

In structuring a new system, two extremes are (1) the players would have their freedom completely returned, leaving all parties free to negotiate financial relationships with whomever they choose, or (2) the players' situation would remain as it is while the owners would have appropriate restrictions imposed on their activities.

Two logical restrictions under the latter plan would require the owners to completely open their operations to player and regulatory scrutiny and to be subject to maximum profit margins (which is, I understand, the plight of most industries granted similar antitrust exemptions), thus preventing the owners from exploiting the monopoly power they have been granted over the players, supposedly for the good of the game.

The players have been forced to give up substantial freedoms while the owners have given up nothing. Equity requires that to correct this situation the players must be made free or the owners must give up an equal dose of their freedom, or some compromise solution between these extremes must be reached. Until such time as an equitable solution can be reached, the strike must continue.

Blaine envisioned nationwide distribution for his essay, so he invested fifty dollars in Xeroxed copies.

"Who in the world are you going to mail it to?" his wife asked.

"Goddamn, . . . you're right," he answered.

Blaine, a member in good standing of the Zero Club, could come up with only two names. The dissertation appeared in Glenn Dickey's column in the San Francisco *Chronicle* and Frank Luksa's column in the Dallas *Times Herald*.

As Blaine intimated, a professional football player in the NFL has the irrelevant free will of a steer wandering through the Fort Worth stockyards. The standard player's contract utilized throughout the league is a chattel agreement rather than a "contract" per se: the player is irrevocably bound to the club; however, the converse is not true. The inherent inequities are best revealed by following the hypothetical career of Theopolis Workman, a black track star from the Sam Yorty Vocational School and Junior College in Libido, California. Workman's career is a composite; all the events are actual.

In his fourth year of junior college, Workman was approached by the Dallas Cowboys as possible free-agent material. Theopolis, flattered that the Cowboys were actually aware of his existence and had even visualized his potential, asked for a pen. In a flash the contracts were executed and Workman was holding a check for a thousand dollars.

"Buy yourself a soda," the scout said as he turned to go.

"Three years?" Workman asked, noticing three separate contracts.

"We don't give three-year contracts to just anybody," the scout replied, using the same line he had used on Cliff Harris several years ago. "See you in training camp," he called out as he drove into the sunset.

Leon Donohue, a real Dallas Cowboy in the mid-sixties, was approached in a similar manner during his senior year at San Jose State.

"Son," the scout said, putting his arm around Donohue, "we'd like to offer you five hundred dollars to sign up and come play with our team."

Leon was flabbergasted. "You mean," he stammered, "you're going to pay me . . . to play football?"

So Theopolis Workman signed as a free agent. His contract specified three years: $13,500 for the first year, $15,000 for the second year, and $16,500 for the third year. Typical free-agent money. "Well," Workman thought, "that's better'n I could make at junior college," and he was right. All Workman had to do to collect his money was make the team.

Elvis Blueberry, Workman's friend and teammate, had been drafted by the Cowboys in the fifth round and understandably fared better in the money department. Blueberry's contract called for three years at $17,000, $18,500, and $20,000, plus a $6,000 bonus. Elvis bought a Pontiac Grand Prix through the Cowboys, and he and Theo drove to training camp.

Upon arrival, Workman and Blueberry joined the eighty other rookies for Coach Landry's keynote address. In the process they were told to familiarize themselves with Paragraph 11 of their player's contract. Paragraph 11 reads:

> Player acknowledges the right and power of the Commissioner (a) to fine and suspend, (b) to fine and suspend for life or indefinitely, and/or (c) to cancel the contract of, any player who accepts a bribe or who agrees to throw or fix a game or who, having knowledge of same, fails to report an offered bribe or an attempt to throw or fix a game, or who bets on a game or who is guilty of any conduct detrimental to the welfare of the league or of professional football. The player, if involved or affected in any manner whatsoever by a decision of the Commissioner in any of the aforesaid cases, hereby releases and discharges the Commissioner, the League, each Club in the League, each Director, Officer, Stockholder, Owner, Partner, employee, agent, official or representative of any Club in the League, jointly and severally, individually and in their official capacities, of and from

> any and all claims, demands, damages, suits, ac-
> tions, and causes of action whatsoever, in law or
> in equity, arising out of or in connection with any
> such decision of the Commissioner.

Theopolis and Elvis failed to realize that by signing the standard player's contract, they had waived their constitutional right to "due process" (guaranteed in the Fifth Amendment), and had agreed to accept Pete Rozelle as judge, jury, and executioner in any behavior deemed "detrimental to . . . professional football." Pete Rozelle is paid over $200,000 per year by the NFL club owners.

As fate would have it, Workman made the team. Unfortunately, his friend Elvis seriously wrenched his knee in a preseason game; it took six weeks for Blueberry to recover fully, and at that point the club released him, citing Paragraph 6 of the standard player's contract. Paragraph 6 states:

> . . . if in the opinion of the Head Coach the player's work
> . . . is unsatisfactory as compared with the work . . . of
> the other members of the Club's squad of players, the
> Club shall have the right to terminate this contract.

Elvis was paid all moneys due, including thirteen dollars per diem for the entire preseason, and two regular-season game checks. Total: $3,263.

"That's all?" Theo was not quite sure what to think. "I thought we had three-year contracts," he said.

"We do," Elvis stated, "but only if the club wants us for three years."

(Catch-22.)

"They're not linked in any way?" Theo asked.

"Nope," Elvis said.

Theopolis Workman went to Gil Brandt and proposed a connection of the contracts as a hedge against permanent disability. In this way Theopolis would be guaranteed a percentage of the payment specified for the remaining two years of his contract if he became seriously injured in his first year.

"We don't want to set a precedent," Gil said, using one of his favorite phrases. "If we do it for you, we've got to do it for forty other guys."

"Oh."

At the end of three good seasons, Workman set about negotiating a new contract. As training camp approached, an impasse was reached with the parties $2,500 apart. Management was firm in their position, so was Workman; he asked to be traded. Workman knew that the Rams and the Packers needed a player of his caliber to strengthen their respective chances for a championship. He waited. Several weeks after his request for a trade, the head coach of the Green Bay Packers phoned Theo.

"You want to play football?" the coach asked.

"Damn right!" Workman said enthusiastically. "I'm ready to go!"

"Then sign with the Cowboys," the coach said. "Your club is asking too much for you; apparently they have no intention of working a trade. Look, I shouldn't be doing this; consider it some friendly advice. If you mention the fact that I called and passed on this information, I'll have to deny every word. . . . You understand, I'm sure."

(Mission: Impossible.)

Theo decided to play out his option. In his personal life he had wrestled with the antebellum racial attitudes indigenous to Dallas for three years; he was ready for a clean break.

"I'll make a deal for myself with the Rams," he said. "It'll be good to get back home."

Workman was benched his fourth season. "Theopolis Workman may not be around next year," Coach Landry stated, "we've got to start replacing him."

When Workman became a free agent the following spring, he found that the Rams and the Packers were not particularly interested in talking with him. There were two reasons: (1) Workman, previously a starting player, had become an unknown quantity because of his inactive fourth season. (2) The Rozelle Rule came into operation. If either the Packers or the Rams signed Theo and would not settle on compensation with the Cowboys, then Commissioner Rozelle would step in and set the compensation. Compensation would be in the form of a player or players, or a future draft selection, whatever Rozelle deemed sufficient. Neither the Rams nor the Packers were willing to risk a commitment requiring indefinite compensation.

Workman, disgusted, signed with the fledgling World Football League.

The World Football League was a rumor in December. With the signings of Csonka, Kiick, and Warfield to the Toronto/Memphis franchise, the League took a quantum leap in status and quickly became a viable alternative for NFL players.

Dallas Cowboys Calvin Hill, Craig Morton, and Mike Montgomery signed immediately to play with the new league in 1975; the reasons were varied. Morton was fed up with his annual selection as the number-two quarterback; through the last several preseasons, Morton and Staubach had battled to statistical draws, yet Staubach, for intangible reasons, invariably won the job. Following last season, Craig asked to be traded; the Cowboys did not respond, so he jumped to the Houston franchise of the WFL. Mike Montgomery was dismayed with the state of player–management relations in Dallas, said as much to the press, and signed a contract with the Birmingham Americans. Calvin Hill was eager for a change in scenery and some big money; he signed with Hawaii.

Those defections, fueled with rumors of further signings, jolted the Cowboy front office into a classic state of overreaction. To reconstruct:

Along about Friday, April 19, Gil Brandt's extensive network of informants regurgitated the name of yet another probable WFL signee: All-Pro Rayfield Wright, perhaps the finest offensive tackle in the game.

Scenario:

"This is unprecedented," Tex Schramm thought as he locked himself in his office and called for the Code Z Emergency File. "A bunch of upstarts are stealing my players."

Eilene Gish, Tex's secretary, dutifully retrieved the file, unlocked the door, and quietly placed the file on Tex's desk. She then tiptoed out of the room. Tex, who had been staring blankly out of his window at the Bryant Heating and Cooling time and temperature sign, wheeled suddenly in his Naugahyde executive's chair and dumped the contents of the file on his desk. The file contained hundreds of 5-by-7-inch index cards, a pithy phrase typed on the face of each. Tex began rummaging. The first card he examined said:

AMERICA: FIX IT OR FUCK IT.

"A holdover from the hippie days," Tex thought. He burned the card in a Dallas Cowboy ashtray.

"This is more like it," he commented after awhile. The card he was holding said:

IF YOU CAN'T STAND THE HEAT, GET OUT OF THE KITCHEN,

but it wasn't quite right.

Twenty minutes later Tex struck gold. "Eureka!" he shouted. This particular card proclaimed:

WHEN THE GOING GETS TOUGH, THE TOUGH GET GOING.

Tex sent the card over to the printer with instructions to reproduce the inscription in a series of decals and one three-color poster. The poster was for Tex's bulletin board; the decals were for the assistant coaches' foreheads.

"We'll show those bastards," Tex said.

In the ensuing legal skulduggery, it never became clear which bastards Tex was after—the World Football League bastards, or his own players.

Late in the evening of Saturday, April 20, Dallas Cowboy attorneys contacted District Court Judge Ted Akin and requested a temporary restraining order to block the World Football League from further contract dealings with Dallas players. Judge Akin: "Their petition claims that the WFL thing is causing irreparable damage and harm to the Dallas Cowboys, and there is a morale factor. They said players who have signed contracts with the WFL won't play as hard because they don't want to take a chance on being hurt. They said it's having a demoralizing effect on other players."

Texas Law requires that there be a "show cause" hearing within ten days of the granting of a temporary restraining order, to determine whether or not the temporary restraining order should become a temporary injunction.

On Saturday afternoon, April 27, Dallas sheriff Clarence Jones summoned a posse. Each deputy was handed a stack of subpoenas and a list of addresses; they were told to deploy and deliver. Thirty-one Dallas Cowboy football players were subpoenaed to appear for the "show cause" hearing in Judge Charles Long's 13th Judicial District Court. The subpoenas instructed the players to bring with them any material relevant to the World Football League. The hearing would be held the following week.

On Wednesday, May 1, Coach Landry, hastily recalled from a European vacation, presented his testimony. In essence, he claimed that the presence of lame-duck players would cause the "quickest disintegration of morale." Gene Stallings took the witness stand the same day and raised doubts about the performance of defecting players. "Maybe he'll miss a pass but be giving a great effort," Gene said, "but the other players may wonder if he tried to catch it. Any time you start doubting a player or coach, you may have disharmony."

On Thursday, Ernie Stautner testified that he felt "strained" talking with defectors. He further stated that he felt hesitant to give them confidential scouting reports on other NFL teams "to help them stock or scout their own [WFL] team."

None of the handful of players who testified ascribed any morale or performance crises to the presence of future WFL players on the Dallas squad.

May 2 was the final day of the hearing, and on that day Judge Charles Long granted a temporary injunction prohibiting the World Football League from signing Dallas Cowboy players. Judge Long's decision was handed down in company with the following dictum:

> It is disturbing that apparently our sense of values and sense of mores have deteriorated as evidenced by, for want of a better expression, "what's in it for me?" The end justifies the means. It is to be regretted that physical ability, a God-given physique, and a proper application of wonderful physical attributes has finally become a matter of barter, purchase, and sale in the market place of today, if you please.

". . . extremely timely and apropos," said Tex Schramm.

"Dictum" is a legal term which in this case translates into the vernacular as "bullshit."

Incidentally, when the United States Government has a case scheduled for a Texas state court (the 134th Judicial District Court, for example) the initial action taken by the Federal attorneys is the removal of the case, by petition, from the state court to a Federal court. The reason for this step is basically simple: the state is not expeditious in its judicial proceedings. State courts are shrouded in a haze of politics; judicial-district judges are elected, political beings, and therefore vulnerable. The crisp, clean action of a Federal court (where judges are appointed for life, confirmed by the Senate, etc.) is not available on a state level.

One significant ramification of Judge Long's granting of a temporary injunction against the WFL was that WFL attorneys were forced to reveal the names of those Cowboy players already under contract to the new league. On July 26, Dallas' excellent wide receiver Otto Stowe revealed his signing with Jacksonville of the WFL. The club reaction was atypically caustic.

Tom Landry: "He doesn't seem to be happy anyplace. He won't be happy in the WFL either. When he wasn't happy in Miami, it was because he wasn't starting. He was starting in Dallas, but the money wasn't enough. Maybe the dollar will make him happy."

Tex Schramm: "I have nothing to say, other than to think our coach took care of it succinctly and to the point."

Stowe was the fourth. Before Judge Long's decision could be overturned by a Civil Appeals Court, the names of three more Dallas players were disclosed. They were D. D. Lewis, a starting linebacker (to play in 1975), Rayfield Wright (1976), and Jethro Pugh (1976). The grand total was seven—a league-leading statistic.

The question which logically arises is, Why? Specifically, why do the Dallas Cowboys lead the entire National Football League in the number and quality of renegade football players? The reasons are abstruse; let us consult an expert, Tex Schramm:

> First, the Cowboys have such a winning tradition and have been such a popular team, not only in Texas but nationally because they've been on television, and our players are so well known that obtaining a Cowboy player brings certain recognition to WFL teams that sign them, as opposed to teams that have been losers.
>
> Secondly, our team would be ripe for these type overtures because our players have accomplished the ultimate in football, winning a world championship. They've enjoyed a great deal of professional success. After you've done that sometimes your goals change. You start capitalizing on what you've accomplished rather than extending your accomplishments.

There might be another motive as far as the Cowboys are concerned. The Cowboys represent success in the NFL. If you're a new league and can attack the symbol of success, that's a pretty good place to start. They wouldn't grab many headlines by stealing players from the Houston Oilers.

There is one other factor. Through the years we've been able to maintain a pretty good morale on our team from a salary standpoint in that we tried, and have been somewhat successful, in keeping an equitable balance. The players are paid in relationship to their contribution to the team. We've always had, as most teams do, players who are not satisfied with their salaries. But I think if you look back on players not satisfied with their salaries, they have not made the point that they weren't being paid fairly in comparison with players on their own team. If they make comparisons, it is with what players on other teams are making.

When the WFL moved in, we faced the possibility of destroying this balance within our own team. Our decision was we could not destroy this balance just because some players might receive offers from WFL teams and other players might not.

Nevertheless, the discouragement factor is great among Cowboy front office personnel. The departing players in some instances were discovered in small, obscure colleges (Pugh at Elizabeth City State, Wright at Fort Valley State), then groomed and refined over a period of years at considerable outlay in time and expense.*

What Tex has offered is a toothless rationale. The foundation of his discussion is the assumption of a calculated

* Tex's comments appeared in the Sunday Magazine, Dallas *Times Herald*, September 15, 1974.

effort on the part of the World Football League to "attack the symbol of success" in the NFL (the Dallas Cowboys) and steal as many of the team's frontline players as possible. That premise is flawed. What Tex does not realize, or refuses to admit, is that the initiative leading to the signings came from each individual Dallas player; all the WFL had to do was exist.

My own situation is a case in point. In the early spring of 1974, the World Football League staged an NFL player draft to establish franchise negotiating rights for veteran NFL players. Although I was selected by the Hawaiian Islanders, I paid little attention, primarily because of the questionable status of the league. My first contact with the club came six weeks after the draft. At that time I spoke with a fellow named Clark Kenyon, a team functionary, and he explained the nature of Hawaii's interest in me. Mike Giddings, formerly a defensive coach with the San Francisco 49ers, had been appointed the Islanders' head coach; he wanted to install Coach Landry's flex defense and he was looking for players who knew the system. He already had Ron East, a one-time Cowboy tackle, and he was interested in both Larry Cole and myself. Kenyon proposed the following terms: three years at $50,000, $55,000, and $60,000, plus a $25,000 bonus—$15,000 to sign, $10,000 upon reporting to training camp. I told Kenyon I'd take two weeks to think it over.

The previous season I had been paid a base salary of $30,000 for my play with the Cowboys, but including preseason and post-season pay, the fulfillment of incentive clauses, and the present value of the NFL pension, the total remuneration had come to approximately $45,000. I extrapolated that figure over the next three years, considering probable raises, and so on, and found that the difference in money was insignificant.

It was late April, and I had yet to hear from the Cowboys on any count: a new contract, my status in the wake of Ed Jones. . . . My sole communication from the club came in the form of a goddamn subpoena. I was suddenly fed up—

with the cybernetic Dallas Cowboys for their impersonal handling of players, and with the Hawaiian Islanders for their pressurized negotiating. I retained two Los Angeles attorneys, Marvin Demoff and Ted Steinberg, to seek out a financially sound WFL team (preferably on the mainland) and negotiate on my behalf. I prepared to play out my option with Dallas.

Now to the root of the "jumping leagues" syndrome. There is an unswerving correlation between the Dallas Cowboys' widespread, generally unspoken, player disgruntlement, and the club's strictly regimented salary structure. As Tex lucidly points out, Cowboy players are paid according to their contribution to the team, *in direct relation to other members of the team.* One is to understand, then, that within the club, the best players are paid the most money; other players fall in line from there (as they should). *However,* the salary ceiling, the amount our best players are paid, is arbitrarily set by Schramm at whatever figure he finds palatable; you either play for that figure, or contend with the politics of playing out your option.

Two years ago the ceiling was in the $45,000–$50,000 range; Jordan, Lilly, Renfro, Staubach, were all drawing salaries more or less in that vicinity. Meanwhile, on other teams, cornerback Lem Barney was drawing in the neighborhood of $65,000; quarterback Greg Landry, over $100,000; Merlin Olsen, over $70,000, to cite just a few examples. Our best players were savagely underpaid, and the rest of the team fell unwittingly into the lowball line; the difference lined the corporate coffers.

The situation presents an unresolvable paradox. I remember one fermented evening in training camp two seasons back. It was 11:30 P.M., the first night out after two grueling weeks of practice. Rayfield Wright was alone on the hall, plaintively wailing, . . . then screaming, "HOW MUCH MORE CAN WE TAKE!!" Rayfield was in the middle of contract negotiations, and he was physically injured; the situation was compounded by several bottles of Boone's Farm Apple Wine. Mel Renfro appeared.

"FRO!" Rayfield shrieked.

Melvin ricocheted down the corridor. "What is it, Cat?" he asked.

"Fro," Rayfield said, "they tell me I'm the best. . . . WHY WON'T THEY PAY ME LIKE THE BBBEEEESSSSTTTTT?"

There was more to Rayfield's frustration than money. A player striving to be successful in professional football derives a certain degree of dignity and self-respect from the process. Players come into the league relatively young, often immature, and grow—in physical ability, but emotionally as well. That is the nature of the game. When you deal with Schramm, Brandt, et al., you are made to feel that dignity and self-respect are imagined qualities: you are a superb physical creation, expertly trained, but in all probability mindless. Many players have been infected with the impression that they are tolerated only because they are necessary pieces in a monumental chess game, a vehicle for the corporate ego.

Larry Cole and I ventured out to training camp in time to watch our second exhibition game, Cowboys versus Rams, in the Los Angeles Coliseum. The ill-fated players' strike, suffocating in its own carbon dioxide, was unofficially over.

"All the players really wanted," Cole said, "was Peace with Honor."

There wasn't even that. The owners were unmerciful; they outflanked the Players Association by telling the rookies they were veterans, and then playing them in the preseason games; a constant barrage of bad press kept the association reeling; and finally, too many name veterans reported.

"It's time to play football," Roger Staubach said.

"God made me do it," John Niland said.

These comments made sports-page headlines.

Training camp is engulfed in ambivalence and lassitude. Rookies have retained beards and long hair; there has been no curfew for them, no singing, and no hauling of ice. Practices have been easy.

"Coach Landry, how about all these bearded rookies?" I asked.

"It's a new erar," he said.

The easy practices ended abruptly with the arrival of the veterans. *A winner never stops proving it* is the cliché of the moment, and Tom has devised a torturous regimen in honor of the new slogan. We are awakened each morning at 6:45 for a leisurely two-to-three-mile run over the semi-mountains that surround the Cal Lutheran campus. Breakfast follows, if you are able to eat. The two-a-day practices are standard fare with one significant new wrinkle: drills are live, with full-speed hitting.

The players, for their part, are not responding. Before one twenty-minute drill a mock vote was taken to determine if there really would be any actual hitting. During the course of the drill, offensive coach Ed Hughes said "Now this is live" thirty-seven times.

Toni Fritsch is having difficulty reconciling his position as a placekicker with the necessity of making the early-morning runs.

"Toni," Coach Landry said, "you will have to learn to do what everybody else does, or go somewhere else and play."

Toni's eyes brightened. "This would be fine," he said.

Cliff and I are rooming together again; our unlikely suite-mates are Lee Roy Jordan and Roger Staubach. I have known Roger only superficially in the past, in part because of the league's hazy caste system (it is commonly realized that good NFL quarterbacks live in a world removed from the rest of us peasants), and because Roger is not easily sifted into component parts. However, the rigors of training camp constitute the necessary centrifuge; some scattered impressions are retrieved:

The most striking thing about Roger is the lack of disparity between his public image and the actual man. Roger is the Clean King. His room is immaculate and comfortable; the bed is always made, toiletries are organized nicely on top of his chest of drawers, a modest radio softly drones. Roger never pads around barefooted, only in slippers; his wardrobe leans to casual double-knits, freshly pressed, of course. I am in awe of his unceasing sparkle.

Roger embodies most of the hackneyed, middle-American values: apples, mom, John Philip Sousa, etc.; God and football run rampant through his life. Staubach is a devout Catholic, fortunately not given to proselytism. He will say "shit" occasionally, but only under extreme duress. It is not remarkable that he hails from Cincinnati, Ohio. Staubach is pigeon-chested, 6 feet 3 inches in height, and he does not fool around on his wife. If he called his own plays (Coach Landry does), he would throw sixty-five passes a game, 80 percent to a double-covered receiver.

Each year Rog makes a token effort at becoming one of the fellows. Two years ago he ingested one shot of tequila at Walt Garrison's birthday party, and vomited heartily. Last year he sampled snuff. Garrison handed Rog a tin of Skoal and Rog took him a big dip. "Not bad," he announced, and went off to a meeting. Now, there is a definite chronological sequence one must follow according to proper snuff-dipping etiquette: (1) you place the dip cleanly in your mouth, and (2) you spit. Roger forgot to spit. He swallowed instead, blushed olive-drab, and vomited many times in succession.

This year Roger plays backgammon with all comers, and steers clear of Walt Garrison.

Last night Staubach, clad only in red boxer shorts, lay innocently in bed reading a worn *Sport* magazine and listening to country music. It was midnight. Mischievous Craig Morton spirited two dandy, drunken foxes into the dorm for a suitable finale to a raucous evening of merriment. The girls, one jolly blonde and one statuesque brunette, stole into Roger's room.

"Oh, my God," Roger said, bolting to his feet.

The girls had him sandwiched, one on each side. The brunette fondled Rog's biceps.

"So you're Roger Staubach," she said.

"Want to see a picture of my wife and kids?" Staubach blurted.

"We don't care about that," the brunette said.

"Yeah," the blonde concurred. ". . . You know, you ain't half bad," she said and patted Roger on the fanny.

It was then Roger noticed his immodest attire. "These, of course, are only basketball shorts," he said, and the girls dissolved in laughter.

Staubach avoided a potentially dangerous situation: he could have been raped.

Morton was fined five hundred dollars for having women in the dormitory.

The first meeting of the 1974 Zero Club proved hopelessly dull. The massive influx of members we envisioned at the club's inception was never materialized; thus spurned, we must once again square with our own vacuous selves.

As a point of conversation, I expressed concern over the presence of Ed Jones; the reams of publicity coupled with the fact that he is playing my position were bothersome.

"Look at it this way," Blaine counseled, "you've got the best fucking defensive lineman in the U. S. of A. . . . BACKING YOU UP. You ought to be flattered."

"Fuck you," I said.

Cole had the season already figured. "You and I will be designated ends to handle only the run," he explained. "We will be called 'Thunder,' and our effective 'pay per play' will double!"

"A-ha," I said. "Ed and Harvey Martin will rush the passer, and eventually become known as "Lightning.' . . ."

"And Lilly and Pugh will be the 'Clap,' " said Blaine.

The prospect of yielding to Harvey (who did an excellent job rushing the passer last year) and Ed in passing situations this season is not a sapid proposition for either Cole or myself. The infiltration of youngsters poses a direct threat to a veteran's territorial imperative; through the years you carve out a position and play it with intensity and pride. Leaving the field intermittently erodes the continuity of your game, diffuses responsibility for the position, and, in the end, destroys the cohesiveness of the defensive unit. Being a run specialist presents another Catch-22: the more effective you are in your job, the less you play.

Something is afoot, however. Gil Brandt and I have finally reached the serious stage of contract negotiations, and the emerging figures are astounding: the Cowboys have tendered a three-year package (three one-year contracts) for some $60,000 per season. The size of the offer indicates a probable shift in personnel, with Ed Jones going over to left end, Cole moving into a tackle position, and Harvey competing for either end slot. The foundation for this assumption is purely economic. If Jones and I are both to play the same position, a gross misallocation of resources would result; no professional football team maintains $500,000-worth of right defensive ends, regardless of amortization. An official confirmation of my assessment would be helpful, of course, but all I can muster from Gil is, "Jones is going to make you a better football player." My inclination is to lie back, and see what develops.

I tromped out to practice this afternoon on the heels of Blaine Nye and John Niland. Blaine is feeling uppity about the team's lackadaisical performance in support of the players' strike and he is delivering to each of the strike-breaking veterans a verbal jab of sarcastic retribution. Today was Niland's turn.

"You fucking scab," Blaine began.

"Nah," John retorted, "as a Christian I had no choice. There's a passage in the Bible that says, 'Slaves, obey your masters; be eager to give them your very best. Serve them as you would Christ.' "

Blaine was confounded by the response; this was his first encounter with John Niland, revitalized. During the past several years Niland has become increasingly difficult to know; his penchant for sudden shifts in life-style has made him something of an enigma within the club. At one time or another John has assumed the mask of a Beau Brummell, a businessman-entrepreneur, an ass-bandit, and a hippie. Today, as a result of a remarkable religious experience which involved eight policemen and Parkland Hospital, John has become a Fundamentalist Christian.

"Gee, that makes it so simple, doesn't it?" Blaine was undaunted. "I mean, God just tells you. . . ."

"No, He doesn't talk to me," John said; "it's a feeling I have. The Bible gives me strength, so I do what it tells me to do."

"What do you mean, it gives you 'strength'?" Blaine asked.

John thought for a moment. "Well, take nasal spray, for instance. I was hooked on nasal spray for seven years, and now I don't need it. . . ."

My contractual discussions with Gil continue. The figure I mentioned earlier, three years at $60,000 per, has finally been agreed to, pending some connection of the three one-year contracts as a hedge against a disabling injury. Gil balked on this point, saying, "We don't want to set a precedent." I spoke with Tex Schramm on the subject and he suggested that it was club policy to pay injured players their due.

"Fine," I said, "let's just firm it up for the record and put it in writing."

"Well," Tex stated, "you'll find that the Cowboys have a history. . . ."

And so forth.

Obviously logic is not going to yield the desired result. My only recourse is the most recent development in sophisticated negotiating artifice—the WFL Bluff. Quite simply, I could urge Gil to come to terms lest I sign with the new league. Unfortunately my bold front would have no foundation. I have nothing substantial to show from the WFL, nor are there any prospects for an attractive contract; I am certain the new league has blown all its ready cash on heavy start-up costs and heady bonus payments to NFL heroes.

Wrong. Steinberg and Demoff, the crack Los Angeles attorneys, arrived this evening with Bill Putnam, owner of the Birmingham Americans, and an awesome contract. Highlights: $50,000 bonus ($25,000 upon signing, $25,000 by April 1, 1975), five connected years at a total of $500,000, limited trade, and no-cut. There are several negative factors: primarily, some of the markets the WFL has seized do not seem viable for the long term, prompting a probability estimate for league survival at less than 50 percent; also, I have uncovered previously undetected emotional ties with the club—if not with the front office and coaching staff, at least with the players. It will be difficult to deliberately uproot myself from a comfortable situation.

All angles considered, I feel the quality of the contract merits a signature.

Following a meeting this morning I visited Coach Landry to inform him of my decision. He led me back into the staff's section of the dormitory and we settled into his office. I opted for a plastic sofa, Tom took a chair facing me; he leaned back, folded his arms and focused his cobalt eyes on my forehead.

"Uh, . . . C-Coach," damn he was staring hard; if he had laser-vision, I would have suffered an immediate pre-frontal labotomy. Start over. Compose yourself.

"Coach, last night I signed with the Birmingham Americans. The decision was a difficult one, but the economics of the situation were overwhelming. . . ."

"Is this your option year?" he asked.

That was a strange question.

"Yes," I answered.

"It's going to be a tough year," he continued. "You've got to realize that if we have a bad season, the defecting players will get most of the blame; . . . there could be a lot of pressure."

Tom went on to discuss his view of the league and the outlook for our season. He signaled the end of the session by standing up.

"Well," he said, "if the league does fail, you'll surface somewhere. You're a pro."

Damn. And all this time I thought I was just an Amateur Drawing Pay.